". . . THE GOOD CONFESSION . . ."
1 Timothy 6:13

Basic Lesson Series—Volume 2

THE
GOOD CONFESSION

"Exercise thyself unto godliness"
1 Timothy 4:7

WATCHMAN NEE

Christian Fellowship Publishers, Inc.
New York

Available from the Publishers at:
11515 Allecingie Parkway
Richmond, Virginia 23235

PRINTED IN U.S.A.

Basic Lessons—Volume 2

CONTENTS

BASIC LESSONS
ON
PRACTICAL CHRISTIAN LIVING

Burdened with the need of a firm foundation for the Christian life, brother Watchman Nee gave a series of basic lessons on practical Christian living during the training session for workers held in Kuling, Foochow, China in 1948. He expressed the hope that these essential lessons might be faithfully learned by God's people, thereby laying a good foundation for the building up of the Body of Christ.

These messages on practical Christian living have now been translated from the Chinese language and will be published in a series of six books, bearing the various titles of: (1) *A Living Sacrifice*; (2) *The Good Confession*; (3) *Assembling Together*; (4) *Not I, But Christ*; (5) *Do All to the Glory of God*; and (6) *Love One Another*.

"Exercise thyself unto godliness" (1 Tim. 4:7), is the exhortation of the apostle Paul. May our hearts be so exercised by God's Word as to give the Holy Spirit opportunity to perfect the new creation.

All quotations of the Scriptures, unless otherwise indicated, are from the American Standard Version of the Bible (1901).

PUBLIC CONFESSION

The Importance of Public Confession

The matter of confession ought to be brought to the attention of new believers as soon as possible. Once a person has trusted in the Lord, he must confess the Lord before men. He should not hide his faith but should publicly confess it. The importance of such confession is both laid down in the Bible and is borne out by our experience.

Suppose a baby makes no sound after one, two, or even three years of age. What would you think? If the child never talks in childhood, most probably he will be dumb for the rest of his life. If he cannot call "Papa," "Mama," as a child, he very likely never will. Likewise, one who believes in the Lord must confess Him immediately, or else he may be dumb throughout his life.

Today we have seen too much of how people can be Christians for ten or twenty years and yet still be mute. Because they are inarticulate during the first and second week of their Christian life, they remain so ever after. The best opportunity to confess the Lord comes right at the be-

1

ginning. If one starts immediately, the way of confession is forever open. So one must force oneself to speak out right after he believes in the Lord, even if he feels it difficult and finds himself rather unwilling. He should confess the Lord before his friends and relatives; otherwise he will be mute for life. We do not want to have any dumb believers; therefore let us learn to open our mouths at the very beginning. Go and find the opportunity to confess our Lord. Confession is a big thing for new believers and a very profitable thing too. If it is not done at the outset, it will become almost impossible later on, unless by the special mercy of God there comes a revival to the soul.

"For with the heart man believeth unto righteousness; and with the mouth confession is made unto salvation" (Romans 10:10). The first half has to do with God while the second half has to do with men. No one can see whether you have believed or not; but if you come to God really believing, you will be justified before Him. Nevertheless, if you believe in your heart but never confess with your mouth, though justified before God, you will not be delivered from the world. The people of this world will not acknowledge you as a saved person. They will still reckon you as one of them, for they have not witnessed any difference between you and them. On this account the Bible emphatically states that besides believing with the heart there must also be confessing with the mouth.

I have seen some people who at first pretended to be Christians but finally turned out to be true Christians. At first they just feigned belief, but as they stood up to declare, "I have believed in Jesus," they became true believers! Many undecided ones, at the time they confess, seal their faith in the Lord. This is comparable to cement

2

which originally is just an easily scattered powder; soon after it is mixed with water, though, it begins to congeal. Many workers have had the experience of seeing people's faith confirmed by saying, "I believe." In preaching the gospel, we help people by pushing, not by pulling. We encourage them to stand up and to confess, "I believe in the Lord Jesus." If anyone confesses with his mouth as well as believes with his heart, he becomes a separated person.

The Advantages of Public Confession

One distinct advantage of publicly confessing the Lord lies in saving the new believer from many, many future troubles. If he does not open his mouth and say that he has followed the Lord Jesus and is now the Lord's, he will always be considered by the world to be one of them. Consequently, whenever they decide to engage in social, sinful, or carnal affairs, they will count him in. For example, when they want to play cards or go to the theater, they will ask him to join them. Why? Because they number him among them. He may sense in his heart that since he is a Christian he should not mix with them, yet he cannot refuse for he desires to please them. Even should he refuse once, undoubtedly he will be asked the second time. Each time he may think of some excuse; yet the problem remains unsettled. How much better it would be if he unfurled the flag on the very first day and confessed that he is a believer. After confessing once or twice, the inroads of the world will be cut.

If a new believer fails to open his mouth and confess the Lord, as a secret Christian he will have ten times as many troubles as an open Christian. His temptations will also be ten times more. He will not be able to free himself from the bondage of human affection and past relationships. He cannot excuse himself every time something comes up by saying he has a headache or is busy. It would be absurd to offer an excuse every time. But if he were to show the flag on the very first day, declaring that formerly he was a sinner but that now he has received the Lord Jesus, all his colleagues, schoolmates, friends and relatives would realize what kind of a person he now is and would not bother him any more. To confess the Lord saves from many troubles.

The Dilemma of Not Confessing

If one fails to confess the Lord, he will be in a wretched plight. Many of those people who believed in the Lord during His earthly days had just such a painful experience. As we know, the Lord Jesus was rejected by the Jews. This rejection was total and the persecution suffered was severe. According to John 9, the Jews agreed that if any man should confess Jesus to be Christ, he should be put out of the synagogue (v. 22). In John 12 it is recorded that many of the Jews believed on the Lord Jesus but did not confess this lest they should be put out of the synagogue (v. 42). They believed secretly but dared not to confess it.

Do you think they could have been at peace about it? No, for though to have confessed the Lord might not have been easy, to not confess Him must have made them even more ill at ease. What kind of a place was the Jewish synagogue? It was where the Jews gathered to oppose the Lord Jesus. It was there that they plotted and conspired to ensnare Him. How could those who truly believed sit among

4

people who schemed against the Lord? With what restraint must they have kept their mouths shut! To speak out was difficult, but to be dumb was not less hard.

This scene in the Jewish synagogue may today be expanded to cover the whole world. People are still questioning and resisting the Lord. They regard Jesus of Nazareth as an enigma. They speak perversely against Him. Under such a situation, how can one who is the Lord's listen to their railings and yet pretend to go along with them? Though to act is both painful and difficult, yet to not act takes all the power the person has to restrain himself. Does he not at heart wish to testify that this man Jesus is the Son of God in whom he has trusted? How can he help but have the inward desire to say: "This Man has saved me; whether you believe Him or not, I do believe."

Alas, many of the rulers among the Jews believed on the Lord Jesus but dared not open their mouths to confess Him for fear of being put out of the synagogue (John 12:42–43). Why do you or anyone else forcibly seal your lips? Is it because you desire to court the friendship of the world or to solicit the sympathy of your relatives or to bid for the respect of men or to seek a position in this world? I often think it would have been much happier for those Jewish rulers if they had confessed the Lord and been cast out of the synagogue. If you have not yet trusted in the Lord, nothing disturbing will happen. But if you are a real believer and yet pretend to be sympathetic to the world, your conscience will undoubtedly be under accusation. How can you have peace in your heart when you witness people sinning while you say with your lips that this is all very interesting? Let me tell you, this is a most agonizing thing for anyone to go through.

5

Suppose we use an illustration. What kind of a person are you if you can sit among people who speak evilly of your mother and you pretend to go along with them? This is contrary to human affection. Likewise, can you keep silent and speak not a word for the Lord who gave His life to save you? Can you refrain from confessing the Lord whom you worship and serve? If this is possible for you, then you are a useless person to the Lord.

Changed Life and Confession

Many new believers, especially those who come from Christian families, have a mistaken idea. They maintain that to confess with their mouths is not essential; what really matters is to shine with good conduct. In other words, their theology is that one's life must change, one's conduct must change; whether his mouth has changed or not does not really matter. We agree with them that should the life remain unchanged, it is futile for the mouth to speak. But we maintain that a changed life without a corresponding confession of the mouth is also useless. Change in conduct is no substitute for confession of the mouth.

New believers should seize the first opportunity to stand up and confess, "I have believed in the Lord Jesus." We must confess with our mouths. If we do not, the world may imagine many things about us. Some may think we have simply been disappointed and hence have taken a pessimistic attitude. Others may consider us as just having had enough of the world; they explain us philosophically without ever touching upon the Lord Jesus. We must therefore stand up and tell them the real reason. Good conduct cannot take the place of confession with the mouth. Good conduct is necessary, but confession is also indispensable. No matter how good one's conduct is, if he has not spoken out for the Lord, his standing is dubious; sooner or later he will be drawn into the whirlpool of this world.

In my many years of labor, I have frequently heard people say: if one's conduct is good, he does not need to open his mouth; what is essential is a good life. But such a saying leaves one loophole; true, no one will speak against one's good conduct, but neither will anyone speak against him even when his conduct is bad. If he had stood up and confessed himself to be Christian, the moment he failed in his conduct, the world would rise up and accuse him. To insist on conduct without confession is actually to provide oneself ground for being poor in conduct and for escaping from being criticized.

Some are afraid to confess the Lord for fear that they may not be able to persevere to the end. They are afraid they will become laughingstocks if after three or four years they quit being Christians. Therefore they would rather wait for a few years; then, after they have proved themselves worthy, they will confess the Lord. To such ones we say: if you dare not confess the Lord for the fear of falling, you surely will fall. Why? Because you have left your back door open; you have already prepared for the day of your fall. It is far better if you stand up and confess that you are the Lord's, for this will shut the back door and make it harder for you to back out. You will then have a better chance to advance rather than to retreat. You can expect to go forward.

Should one wait for better conduct before he confesses the Lord, most probably he will never in his life open his

7

mouth. He will be dumb even after his conduct is good. It is most difficult to open one's mouth if one does not do so at the very beginning.

One fact should comfort us, and that is, God is the God who keeps us as well as the God who saves us. What is it to be saved? It is like purchasing something. What is it to be kept? It is like keeping the thing in hand. Who would ever buy something in order to throw it away? If you buy a watch for yourself, it is because you are thinking of using it. You do not buy it that you may throw it out. Likewise, when God purchases us, it is to keep us. God redeems us in order to keep us. He will keep us until that day. He so loves us as to give up His Son for us. Had He not meant to keep ʾus, He would never have paid such an immense price. Keeping is God's purpose; keeping is God's plan. Do not, therefore, be afraid to rise up and confess. You do not need to worry about tomorrow, for God will worry for you. All you need to do is to stand up and confess in simplicity that you belong to God. Just throw yourself into His hand. He knows when you need succor and He will comfort and preserve you. We have the greatest confidence in proclaiming that God keeps those whom He has saved. Redemption would be meaningless if it were without preservation.

A Reason for Not Confessing

Why do we not confess the Lord? Other than the reason we have already mentioned, the fear of not persevering, the most common reason is the fear of man. Many Christians really do have a desire to stand up and confess the Lord, but as soon as they look at people's faces, they dare not say anything. A look at their parents' countenances or their friends' faces makes them hesitant. They are afraid of man, so they do not have the courage to open their mouths. Perhaps they are naturally timid. For them to stand up before man and say, "I have believed in the Lord," is like taking their life from them. Such fear is a real hindrance to spiritual life.

"The fear of man bringeth a snare" (Prov. 29:25). As one fears, one falls into a snare. Fear itself is a snare. It is a self-planted snare, laid by the fear in the person. Let such a person realize that the one whom he fears might like to hear what he has to say; and even if he doesn't, he may not be as fearful as imagined.

I recall a story: once there were two men who worked in the same firm. One of the two got saved. Now both men were extremely timid. The one who got saved dared not tell the other that he was saved, while the other could not work up enough courage to ask the saved one what had happened, though he could see the change. They shared the same table at work. Daily they faced each other. Yet one dared not tell and the other dared not ask. One day the one who had believed could stand it no longer. So after much prayer he went to his friend, took the latter's hand and said, "I am a most timid person. For at least three months I have not dared tell you something. Now I am going to tell you that I have already believed in the Lord Jesus." His face turned pale while he spoke. Then his friend answered, "It has been three months since I wanted to ask you what had happened."

He who fears man falls into a snare. Let him remember: as he is in fear of others, probably others are in fear of him too. A new believer ought not to have the fear of man. All who follow God must be fearless. If there is fear, one cannot be a good Christian nor can he serve God. We must be bold in confessing the Lord before men both in private and in public. From the very start, we must help young believers to go this way.

Confession Breaks the Sense of Shamefulness

People are not only afraid, they are sometimes shy. I think many of God's children have to acknowledge that they have an unnecessary sense of shamefulness before the world. Why should we feel shameful in confessing ourselves to be Christians? Such unreasonableness needs to be completely broken. Let us solve it by considering two points.

The first point is: when the Lord Jesus was hanged on the cross, He bore our shame as well as our sins. The Bible clearly teaches that He was put to shame. He was humiliated by the soldiers at Calvary. If we suffer disgrace from men, it is our rightful portion. Any mortification we receive from men today can never be compared with the shame which our Lord endured on the cross. Let it be no surprise to us to suffer shame, for this is the portion of all who belong to the Lord.

The second point is: the world, not us, ought to be ashamed. There is a poem which runs like this: "Can a flower be ashamed of the sun? As a flower opens to the sunlight, so will we confess the Lord. The world, not we, ought to feel ashamed." Can we be ashamed of confessing Him who has so graciously saved us? Can we do that—any more than the flowers can be ashamed of the sun that sustains them? How can we deny the One who has succored

10

us and led us to heaven? Do we consider all the grace which He has bestowed upon us as ignominious? The Lord has done so much for us; is it shameful to confess Him? No, there is absolutely no possibility of being ashamed to confess Him.

How true is the poem: the world, not we, ought to feel ashamed. We too declare that the world is shameful both now and forever. Today the people of this world live in sin, but, thank God, we have been separated. They, not we, walk according to the lusts of the flesh. They are under bondage, while we are free. They do the hidden things of shame which we renounced. They follow the evil spirit that works in them, but we are completely delivered. So the shame is theirs, not ours.

To confess the Lord is nothing to be ashamed of; it is, rather, a joyous and glorious matter. So far as the future is concerned, they of the world will suffer punishment, even eternal destruction from the face of the Lord and from the glory of His might. But we who follow the Lamb shall be with Him forevermore. How wrong it is for people to heap shame on us. Theirs is the shame, not ours. We should stand up boldly and proclaim that we gladly and gloriously belong to God.

Why were the rulers in John 12 afraid to confess the Lord? Because they loved the glory of men more than the glory of God (v. 43). They were bashful because they sought the glory that comes from men. All who wish to follow the Lord ought neither be afraid nor bashful. If light is shameful while darkness is glorious, if holiness is shameful while sinfulness is glorious, if spirituality is shameful while carnality is glorious, if following the Lord is shameful while human degradation is glorious, then we would

11

rather choose to be ashamed. Let us be like Moses, counting the reproach of Christ greater riches than the glory of men.

Truth Is Absolute

Another point yet to be mentioned is that the synagogue represented much. Why did so many dare not confess? For the simple reason that they wished to have both Christ and the synagogue. If they did not want Christ, all they needed to do was just to refuse to believe; if they did not desire the synagogue, they could simply confess the Lord. But should they wish for both, their lips would be sealed. Wishing for both reveals the lack of absoluteness.

Whether or not we are persecuted by the world after believing, let us yet thank the Lord. We should not cling to the synagogue like those rulers of old, daring not to confess that we are believers. Let me tell you one thing: if everyone in the church were like those rulers, there would be no Christianity today. The synagogue would be preserved, but the church would be missing. If Peter and Paul and Luther had returned home without saying a word about their faith in the Lord, they no doubt would have had less trouble, but where would the church be today?

It is a characteristic of the church to boldly confess the Lord as well as to believe in Him. To be saved means more than believing; it also includes confessing. Such confession of the Lord is most important in Christianity. We must speak out or there will be no Christianity! The Word of God is clear: "For with the heart man believeth unto righteousness, and with the mouth confession is made unto salvation" (Rom. 10:10). In the church, not one believer but every believer must walk in this way of confession. We should not let anyone fall short in this matter. The church will be strong if all are confessing their faith; otherwise it will be weak.

Our Confession and the Lord's Confession

"Every one therefore who shall confess me before men, him will I also confess before my Father who is in heaven" (Matt. 10:32). How we thank the Lord for His confessing us in the future if we confess Him today. Today, before men who are as the grass of the field, we confess Him as Jesus Christ, the Son of the Living God, but on that day when our Lord shall come back He will confess us before His Father and before His angels in glory. If we feel it difficult to confess Him today, will He find it hard to confess us in that day?

"But whosoever shall deny me before men, him will I also deny before my Father who is in heaven" (Matt. 10:33). How great is the contrast! If we find it burdensome to confess before men that we have a Man who is above all men, a Man who is truly the Son of Man, how will He confess us before His Father when He shall come with His angels in glory—us who are so ragged? This indeed is a serious matter. Please remember that in comparison to His confessing us one day, our confessing Him is not at all difficult. For Him to confess us is mystifying—for we are but prodigal sons coming home. We have absolutely nothing in ourselves. Let us, then, all the more ardently confess Him, since we know that He will one day confess us.

Peter was a heroic type of person, one who must occupy the first place among men. He dared to do anything. He was a hero. But on a certain day, he was as timid as a mouse. In response to a simple question he lost his courage and dared not confess the Lord. He was afraid to confess before a slave girl, a person who had no freedom of her own. What indecency for Peter, a natural hero and leader, to flee even before a sword had been drawn, to be afraid before anyone even wanted his life, and to tremble and swear in the presence of a slave girl! Shame on Peter and shame on him for swearing with a curse.

Shame on all who do not have the courage to open their mouths. Glory belongs to those who dare to confess the Lord Jesus, whether through fire or through water. Nothing on earth is more admirable than such confession. To be scourged, to be thrown into fire, or to be cast into the lion's den while still confessing, "I belong to Jesus of Nazareth"—this is the world's most glorious sight. It is most shameful for any believer not to mention the Lord Jesus before men. Such a person is totally useless. He will even abhor himself and acknowledge his conduct as most shameful.

It is our sincere hope that young believers will at the outset dare to confess whose they are. Do not ever try to be a hidden Christian. If young believers walk well in this way of confession, they will become useful to God. May God lead us further on.

SEPARATED FROM THE WORLD

There are a great number of commands, examples, and teachings in the Bible concerning the matter of separation. Since the world has so many facets to it, our separation needs to be full and complete. There are four different places in the Bible used to typify the world: Egypt represents the pleasures of the world; Ur of Chaldea, the religion of the world; Babylon, the confusion of the world; and Sodom, the sins of the world. From all of these we need to be separated.

And Moses and Aaron were brought again unto Pharaoh: and he said unto them, Go, serve Jehovah your God; but who are they that shall go? And Moses said, We will go with our young and with our old; with our sons and with our daughters, with our flocks and with our herds will we go; for we must hold a feast unto Jehovah. And he said unto them, So be Jehovah with you, as I will let you go, and your little ones: look to it; for evil is before you. Not so: go now ye that are men, and serve Jehovah; for that is what ye desire. And they were driven out from Pharaoh's presence.

Ex. 10:8–11

And Jehovah said unto Moses, Stretch out thy hand toward heaven, that there may be darkness over the land of Egypt, even darkness which may be felt. And Moses stretched forth his hand toward heaven; and there was a thick darkness in all the land of Egypt three days; they saw not one another, neither rose any one from his place for three days; but all the children of Israel had light in their dwellings. And Pharaoh called unto Moses, and said, Go ye, serve Jehovah; only let your flocks and your herds be stayed: let your little ones also go with you. And Moses said, Thou must also give into our hand sacrifices and burnt-offerings, that we may sacrifice unto Jehovah our God. Our cattle also shall go with us; there shall not a hoof be left behind; for thereof must we take to serve Jehovah our God; and we know not with what we must serve Jehovah, until we come thither.

Ex. 10:21–26

And ye shall keep it until the fourteenth day of the same month; and the whole assembly of the congregation of Israel shall take of the blood, and put it on the two side-posts and on the lintel, upon the houses wherein they shall eat it. And they shall eat the flesh in that night, roast with fire, and unleavened bread; with bitter herbs they shall eat it. Eat not of it raw, nor boiled at all with water, but roast with fire; its head with its legs and with the inwards thereof. And ye shall let nothing of it remain until the morning; but that which remaineth of it until the morning ye shall burn with fire. And thus shall ye eat it: with your loins girded, your shoes on your feet, and your staff in your hand; and ye shall eat it in haste: it is Jehovah's passover.

Ex. 12:6–11

And the children of Israel journeyed from Rameses to Succoth, about six hundred thousand on foot that were men, besides children. And a mixed multitude went up also with them; and flocks, and herds, even very much cattle. And

16

they baked unleavened cakes of the dough which they brought forth out of Egypt; for it was not leavened, because they were thrust out of Egypt, and could not tarry, neither had they prepared for themselves any victuals. Now the time that the children of Israel dwelt in Egypt was four hundred and thirty years. And it came to pass at the end of four hundred and thirty years, even the selfsame day it came to pass, that all the hosts of Jehovah went out from the land of Egypt. It is a night to be much observed unto Jehovah for bringing them out from the land of Egypt: this is that night of Jehovah, to be much observed of all the children of Israel throughout their generations.

Ex. 12:37–42

Wherefore
   Come ye out from among them, and be ye
      separate,
saith the Lord,
   And touch no unclean thing;
   And I will receive you.

2 Cor. 6:17

Meaning of Redemption Typified by the Exodus from Egypt

When the Israelites were in the hand of the destroyer, how did God deliver them? It was by the paschal lamb. At the time the angel of God went through the land of Egypt to smite the first-born, he passed over those houses which had blood on them. If there were no blood on the door, he went in and smote the first-born. Thus, the whole question of salvation does not depend on whether or not the door is good, the doorposts are special, the household is commendable, or the first-born is obedient. It rather hinges on whether there is blood. The difference between salvation

17

and perdition is determined by acceptance or rejection of the blood. The basis for your salvation is not in what you or your family are, but in the blood.

We who are saved by grace are redeemed by the blood. Let us remember, however, that once we have been redeemed by the blood, we must start to make our exit. The Israelites killed the lamb before midnight and, after they had put the blood on the doorposts and the lintel, they hurriedly ate their meal. As they ate, they had their loins girded, their shoes on their feet and their staves in their hands, for they were ready to go out of Egypt.

The first effect of redemption, therefore, is separation. God never redeems anyone and leaves him in the world to live on as before. Every regenerated person, as soon as he is saved, needs to take his staff in his hand and start to make his exit. As soon as the angel of destruction separates between those who are saved and those who are perishing, the saved souls must go out. This is most clearly typified in Exodus. A staff is used for journeying; no one uses it as a pillow for lying down. All the redeemed, both big and small, must take their staves and move out that very same night. Whenever souls are redeemed by the blood, they become pilgrims and strangers in this world. The moment they are redeemed, they leave Egypt and are separated from the world. They ought not continue to abide there.

Once a sister in the Lord was teaching the children. She told them the story of the rich man and Lazarus. She put a question to these youngsters: "Whom would you choose to be—Lazarus or the rich man? The rich man enjoys life today but suffers later on, while Lazarus suffers now but has enjoyment hereafter." A little girl about eight years old stood up and answered: "When alive I want to be the

18

rich man, but after death I want to be Lazarus." Many today are like that little girl. When I am in need of salvation, I trust in the blood of the Lamb; but after I am saved, I prefer to stay put in Egypt. I want both.

Nonetheless, we must remember that to be redeemed by the blood is to be delivered from the world. Once redeemed, instantly we become pilgrims and sojourners on earth. This does not imply that we no longer live on earth; it simply means we are instantaneously separated from the world. Wherever there is redemption, there is separation. The blood divides the living and the dead; the blood separates God's children from the people of the world. The redeemed are no longer permanent residents of this world.

It does not take several years for the redeemed to be separated. On the very same night that one is redeemed, he is separated from the world. No one can boast that after several days' deliberation he decided to come out of the world. If he is a Christian, he belongs to the Lord and ought to leave Egypt (the world) immediately.

From the way the Israelites left Egypt, we can see how difficult it was for them to make their exit, for Egypt held on to them. Even after Pharaoh agreed to let them go, he demanded that only the men should go, that the little ones and the old ones should remain behind. How could the men go far if their little ones and old folks stayed behind in Egypt? No doubt the men would soon return. The wile of Satan was to prevent a thorough and total separation from Egypt. Moses therefore rejected such contrivance from the very outset. Let us remember, if we leave one thing or one person behind, we will not be able to go very far but will eventually return to the world.

We recall that the above demand was not the only one

19

Pharaoh made of the Israelites. Earlier he called for Moses and said, "Go ye, sacrifice to your God in the land" (Ex. 8:25); that is, worship God in Egypt, do not go into the wilderness. Later on, he tried to persuade the people of God not to go very far away (8:28). Still later, he asked that only the men go but that the little ones and the old ones remain behind (10:11). And lastly, he conceded to let the little ones go but insisted that the flocks and herds stay (10:24). The basic thinking of Pharaoh was that if they must be God's people, let them be His people in Egypt. He knew very well that they could not have a good testimony by serving God in Egypt. Those who served God in Egypt would also serve Pharaoh. They would be Satan's servants as well as God's.

Do you desire to serve God and remain in the world? You will without doubt be Satan's servant and make bricks for him. He will not let you go, nor will he allow you to go far away. He may permit the men to go but keep the rest in Egypt, for he knows they will come back. He is fully acquainted with the teaching in Matthew 6:21: "For where thy treasure is, there will thy heart be also." The treasure and the person are always together. He is certain that you will not go far if your flocks and herds are left behind. Soon you will come seeking the flocks and the herds. But God wants the flocks and the herds to go with you. Your wealth, your money, must also be delivered with you.

When we go out to the wilderness, we must bring all our property with us. God's command is clear: we who serve God must be separated from the world.

Our Way Is in the Wilderness

To confess the Lord Jesus with our mouth alone is not enough; we must also come out of the world and be separated. This is a step further than confession. Certainly we should not be silent Christians, but words alone are insufficient. We must be separated people. We need to see and to treasure the new position we now have in the Lord; we must leave our former position far behind. We cannot maintain our former friendships, affections, and relationships. We must go out with all our things. People may consider us foolish, but we must go out of the world. Since we have become Christians, our way lies in the wilderness, not in Egypt.

According to the New Testament sense, both Egypt and the wilderness represent the world. Egypt, however, points to the world in its moral sense while the wilderness speaks of the world in its physical sense. We Christians are in the physical world but not in the moral world. The world, as we know it, is a system as well as a place. Egypt stands for the system in which there are so many attractive things to draw out the lusts of the eyes, the lusts of the flesh, and the pride of life. The wilderness symbolizes the place in which we live.

We Christians must come out of the world as a system. To be separated from the world means to be separated from this world system in its moral connotation. It does not imply leaving the world as a place.

D. M. Panton has a well-spoken word concerning our walk in the wilderness. He says: in life, it is a way; in death, it is a tomb. No one can remain in this world too long, for it is only a way. It also serves as a grave when one dies. This should be our attitude towards the world. Every believer must be separated. In the eyes of the people of this world, we are but strangers and sojourners in the wilderness; they alone are the permanent residents of the world.

Let me use an illustration to show the meaning of separation. During the latter part of my stay in England, shortly before the Munich Pact was signed under the appeasement policy of Prime Minister Chamberlain, I noticed people busily preparing for war by digging trenches, constructing airfields, building shelters and even distributing masks for poisonous gas. My feeling at that time was entirely different from that of the Englishmen. I watched them prepare for war; I saw them collect contributions and train their home guards. Then one night the telegram came saying that the pact was signed and there was no need to fear war. Many could not sleep that night. They sang and they shouted. But what was my reaction? Three words sum up my feeling: I watched coldly. While they had been busily preparing for war, I had watched coldly; now when they were joyous with peace, I watched coldly. Why? Because I was a sojourner, I would soon go away. Since I was but a traveler in England, my feeling was totally different from that of the Englishmen. In their joy and in their sorrow, I was merely an observer. Thus it was I truly realized what it meant to be an alien.

Although we have not yet left this world as a place, we have already departed from it as a system. Morally speaking, we do not belong. Unless we can look back at the world as having left it, we are wrong. Unless we can observe it coldly, we have fallen. If we cannot adopt a spectator's attitude towards all the things and all the relationships in the world, we have failed as Christians. It shows that we are still in it and have yet to come out.

While I was in England I naturally hoped for peace, but I was not disturbed by the rumors of war. I too hoped there would be no bombing, but was not greatly concerned. Once I told a brother, "God saved me to be a Christian, not an Englishman." I could not help feeling that way for God had saved me to be a Christian. My attitude towards England was neutral: I hoped for her good, I wished her peace; but my interests lay elsewhere.

Young believers should see that, as Peter and other apostles put it, we are but sojourners and pilgrims on this earth. We have already come out of the world system. Those of the world wish to retain us, draw us closer to them, keep us and our possessions back, but we cannot serve God if we yield at any one point.

Henceforth let our faces turn towards the promised land. We are separated from Egypt. The blood makes the separation, for the blood has redeemed us to God. Those unredeemed by the blood are the Egyptians. The unredeemed belong to the world, but the redeemed have become citizens of another world.

Suppose you go to a store to buy a watch. After buying, you leave with it. You do not give the watch to the storekeeper and ask him to use it. No, you buy it and you leave with it. Where there is buying, there is leaving. Do remember that the blood has bought us that we may leave the world system. Everyone who is bought by the blood leaves. We are bought to follow the Lord and to travel towards the promised land.

Principles Governing Separation

Some probably will ask: from what should we come out? What are the things of the world? Wherein must we be separated from the world? We shall suggest five principles of separation. But before going into these principles, there is one thing needed first: we need to have our heart and spirit released from the world first. If anyone still desires to be in the world, these principles will be of no avail to him. Even if he separates himself from a hundred things, he is yet in the world. Separation of the person with his heart and his spirit must precede the separation of things.

The man must completely come out of Egypt and be separated from the world. Do not be afraid to be called peculiar. There are things we have to deal with and there are ways in which we ought to be different from the world, even though we desire to be at peace with all men. In our homes, in the office, or wherever we may be, we contend not. We are not belligerent to anyone. But still there are a few things from which we must be separated.

1. THINGS WHICH THE WORLD CONSIDERS UNWORTHY OF A CHRISTIAN

We must be separated from anything the world considers unworthy of a Christian. We start our Christian life before the world and the world sets up certain standards for Christians. If we cannot measure up to their standards, where will our testimony be? Of the things which we do, we should never permit non-believers to raise their eyebrows saying, "Do Christians do such things too?" Under such an accusation, our testimony before them is finished. For example: Suppose you visit a certain place and meet a non-Christian there. He murmurs, "Do you Christians visit this place?" There are many places non-believers may frequent and be quite able to defend their action when questioned. But if a Christian should go to those same places, immediately they will raise an objection. They may sin, but you cannot. They may do it without any problem, but if you do the same thing you will be criticized. Consequently, whatever the world condemns as unworthy of a Christian, we must not do. This is a minimum requirement.

I know of many sons and daughters who have non-believing parents. If they ask their parents for this and that thing, I have heard the parents say, "Since you have believed in the Lord Jesus, do you still ask for these things?" Let me tell you; to be corrected by the non-believing world is disgraceful for Christians. Abraham was reproved by Abimelech for his lie. This is one of the most shameful things recorded in the Bible. Non-believers may lie, but do we lie also? Things which the Egyptians consider as unworthy of us we must be separated from.

2. THINGS WHICH ARE INCONSISTENT TO OUR RELATIONSHIP WITH THE LORD

Anything which is inconsistent to our relationship with the Lord must be rejected. Our Lord was humiliated on earth; can we seek for glory? He was crucified as a robber; can we court the favor of this world? He was slandered as possessed of a demon; can we look for praise from men that we are most clever and rational? Such conditions reveal the inconsistency of our relationship with the Lord. They make us different from the Lord, even contrary to Him. All the ways which He has gone we also must walk through. For this cause we must eradicate everything that is inconsistent to our relationship with the Lord.

"A disciple is not above his teacher, nor a servant above his lord" (Matt. 10:24), says the Lord. This refers to our relationship with the world, showing how we must suffer slander and reproach. If they treated our Lord that way, can we expect to be treated differently? If this is the way they dealt with our teacher, can we hope for anything different? If we *are* treated differently, something must be drastically wrong in our relationship with the Lord. Let us be careful that along with other children of God, we walk together in the way of the Lord. Whatever conditions our Lord faced on this earth, we must also follow.

All who follow Jesus of Nazareth should be prepared for disgrace, not for glory. Whoever follows Him must be ready to bear the cross. The first time people meet the Lord, they do not hear Him say, "Behold, how glorious it is!" Rather they hear Him say, "If any man would come after me, let him deny himself, and take up his cross, and follow me" (Matt. 16:24). He speaks these words at the gate of entrance, not in the inner chamber. He has forewarned us that He calls us to bear the cross. This is our way, the only way to follow the Lord. His relationship to the world is our relationship to the world. We must keep our oneness with the Lord.

"But far be it from me to glory, save in the cross of our Lord Jesus Christ, through which the world has been crucified unto me, and I unto the world" (Gal. 6:14). The cross stands between the world and the Lord. By the cross, we stand on the Lord's side. On one side is the Lord, on the other side is the world; standing in between is the cross. Our attitude towards the world is defined by the cross. The world has given the cross to our Lord, so it stands on the other side. Since we are on the Lord's side, we cannot go over to the world except through the cross. But the cross cannot be passed over, for it is an accomplished fact, a matter of history. We are not able to eliminate fact or cancel history. The world has crucified our Lord on the cross; how can we bypass the cross? Since the cross is a fact, to us the world being crucified on it will always be a fact. If there is no way to dismiss the cross, there can be no possibility of abolishing the fact that the world has been crucified. Unless we are able to delete the cross, we cannot go over to the other side, the world side. Thank God, we are on this side of the cross.

To illustrate: if a man's father or mother or brother is murdered, he will refuse to come to terms with his foe. His dear one has been killed, so what ground is there left for talking? Before the killing, the whole thing was open for discussion; but after the killing, there is nothing to be talked about. Likewise, the cross has now become factual. What more can we say? The world has crucified our Lord on the cross, so we now stand on the Lord's side and declare that so far as the world is concerned, we are crucified and as far as we are concerned, the world is crucified. Today there can be no communication between the two. The world cannot cross over to our side, nor can we cross over to the world.

Having seen the cross, we glory in it. Through the cross "the world hath been crucified unto me, and I unto the world" (Gal. 6:14). These two stand on opposite sides. Whatever men may say, the cross is an historical fact. It cannot be changed. The Christians are on one side, the world is on the other side, and the cross is in between.

27

When we open our eyes, we see the cross, not the world. If ever we see the world, we see the cross first. We can retort with anger even as the one whose father or mother or brother was killed, and say, there is nothing to talk about.

Young Christians must be brought to see that the Lord's position is also theirs. Frequently they ask: will I touch the world if I do such and such? Can I do this or can I do that? It is very hard for us to explain everything to them, but we can give them a principle. We can tell them that even as the world and the cross are opposite to each other, so are the world and our Lord. If they go to the Lord with an open and tender heart, they will clearly see the difference in these two sides.

What is the world? What is not the world? You will know when you come to the Lord. You need only ask one question: how was this thing related to the Lord Jesus while He was on earth? What was the relationship of the Lord to the people of the world? If your relationship is not different from Christ's, it is good. But if your position differs from His, it is wrong. We are followers of the Lamb who has been slain. We follow the Lamb whithersoever He goes (Rev. 14:4). We stand together with the Lamb in His slain position. Whatever does not stand in that position, whatever is contrary to the Lord's position, is the world from which we must be separated.

3. THINGS WHICH QUENCH SPIRITUAL LIFE

Again we ask, "What is the world?" Each and everything which tends to quench our spiritual life before the Lord is the world. How impossible it is to tell new believers what things are permissible and what things are not permissible. If we tell them ten things, they have the eleventh thing to ask. But if they understand but one principle, they can apply it to numberless things. Whatsoever thing makes you lose zeal for prayer or for Bible reading or causes you to lose courage to testify is the world.

The world creates a kind of atmosphere which cools our love to the Lord. It withers our spiritual life; it chills our zeal; it freezes our longing for God. Hence it must be rejected.

Can things which are not sinful be reckoned as things of the world? Many things rate highly in human estimation; but the question is, do they help us draw nearer to the Lord? Or will they quench our spiritual life? Indeed, they may be good things, yet in doing them several times, our inner fire begins to dwindle; if we continue in them, the fire soon becomes cold. We find ourselves unable to confess our sins, to pray and to read the Bible. Though these worldly things may not have occupied our time, they surely have occupied our conscience. They have weakened our conscience before God and given us an unspeakable sense of being wrong. Our conscience cannot rise above that feeling. It takes away our taste for the Bible. It makes us feel empty when we wish to testify. It swallows up our words. No matter how sinless these things are, how very right they may be, they still must be labeled as the world. All that which quenches our spiritual life belongs to the world.

4. Social Affairs Which Hinder the Testimony

Another thing to be mentioned is concerned with social relationships. Whatever social gatherings or feasts or good times together cause our lamp to be covered under a bushel are of the world. These should be rejected. How can Christians continue in social intercourse if they cannot confess that we are the Lord's and if they have to pretend to be polite by listening to and smiling with unbelievers? How can we suppress our inward feeling and put on a smiling face? How can we inwardly sense the world, yet show sympathy outwardly? How can we judge anything sinful, if we externally agree with it? Many of God's children have been gradually drawn back into the world because they failed to differentiate in their social life.

Beginners in Christ must be clear of their position at the start. The right choice needs to be made. It is not that we wilfully refrain from having communication with others. We are not John the Baptists who eat not and drink not. We follow the Lord in both eating and drinking. We are not ascetics; we do have dealings with men. But, we must maintain our position. People must not be allowed to interfere with our Christian position. They should respect our position. Though sometimes they may disapprove, they cannot change it.

When social contacts affect our testimony, we know it is the world. In our dealings with men, we should be able to manifest our Christian position. Otherwise, it is better for us to be separated. "Nor standeth in the way of sinners, nor sitteth in the seat of scoffers" (Ps. 1:1), says the psalmist. If we walk in the way of sinners, we will soon be where they are. If we sit with the scoffers, we will quickly be contaminated with ungodliness. Both sin and ungodliness are highly contagious; we must flee from them as fleeing from the plague.

5. THINGS WHICH WEAK BELIEVERS CONDEMN

Whatever thing causes the conscience of weak believers to stumble is to be taken as the world. At the outset we mentioned things condemned by the world as unworthy of Christians; now we speak of things condemned by feeble Christians. Notice these are not things disapproved of by strong Christians; rather they are reprehended by weak Christians. As a matter of fact, these weak believers may not be correct in their judgment. What they disapprove of may be quite all right. Yet they have a weak conscience just as once we did. How can I stumble them in the things which they consider wrong? I must walk before them as without any offense. "All things are lawful for me; but not all things are expedient" (1 Cor. 6:12), says Paul. All things are lawful, for from our standpoint these things are not of the world, but to feeble Christians they are things of the world. Consequently we must for their sake refrain from them.

Paul uses an extreme case to illustrate this point. He says, "If meat causeth my brother to stumble, I will eat no flesh for evermore, that I cause not my brother to stumble" (1 Cor. 8:13). It is not easy to abstain from meat, especially when Paul in his letter to Timothy writes, "Some shall fall away from the faith . . . to abstain from meats, which God created to be received with thanksgiving by them that believe and know the truth" (1 Tim. 4:1, 3). But Paul is willing to go to extremes. Whether to eat meat or not is a small matter to him; his followers, though, may not have the same knowledge. He knows when to stop, but those who follow him may walk a few steps too far. If he eats meat, they may go to the heathen temple and partake of meats sacrificed to idols and later fall into idolatry. We must, therefore, be careful in whatever things feeble Christians consider as of the world, even if they have no real relationship with it.

Come Out from the World

"Wherefore come ye out from among them, and be ye separate, saith the Lord, and touch no unclean thing; and I will receive you, and will be to you a Father, and ye shall be to me sons and daughters, saith the Lord Almighty" (2 Cor. 6:17–18). This is the first time in the New Testament where the name "the Lord Almighty" is used. We shall find it later in the book of Revelation. In Hebrews, it is "El Shaddai." "El" means God, "Shaddai" has its root in the word which means a woman's breast or milk. Hence this name should be translated as the All-Sufficient God. What a child needs is milk, and this milk comes from the mother's breast. So the mother's breast supplies all the needs of a child. So is our God.

The Lord as the All-Sufficient God calls us to come out from the world and touch not the unclean things that He may receive us as sons and daughters. These are not mere words, for they are supported by the All-Sufficient God. If we leave all, we shall be empty-handed, but He will receive us.

Let it be known that all who have been received by the Lord have been separated from the world. Many do not sense the preciousness of the Lord because they have not counted all things as refuse. Negatively speaking, those who do not count all things as refuse must necessarily look on earthly things as treasures; therefore they do not know what it means to be received of God. How we need to know the Father as the All-Sufficient One.

"When my father and my mother forsake me, then Jehovah will take me up" (Ps. 27:10). Again, "My flesh and my heart faileth; but God is the strength of my heart and my portion forever" (Ps. 73:26). Who can experience such sweetness? Only those who have come out, who have forfeited all. The blind man who was healed found the Lord after he was cast out of the synagogue. If we remain in the synagogue, we will not meet the Lord. If we are driven out, we shall have the blessing of the Lord upon us. How precious this is! Come out, therefore, and taste the sweetness of the Lord!

THE ELIMINATION
OF DISTINCTIONS

After having confessed the Lord before men and having been separated from the world, new believers should be shown that all believers are one in the body of Christ. We may call this the elimination of distinctions.

"For in one Spirit were we all baptized into one body whether Jews or Greeks, whether bond or free; and were all made to drink of one Spirit" (1 Cor. 12:13). The word "whether" implies that all distinctions have been eliminated. In the body of Christ, there can be no earthly discriminations. We are all baptized in one Spirit to be one body, and then we are all made to drink of one Spirit.

"For as many of you as were baptized into Christ did put on Christ. There can be neither Jew nor Greek, there can be neither bond nor free, there can be no male and female; for ye all are one in Christ Jesus" (Gal. 3:27–28). Those in Christ are those who have clothed themselves with Christ. The natural distinctions of Jew and Greek, bond and free, male and female have been abolished.

"And have put on the new man that is being renewed unto knowledge after the image of him that created him:

where there cannot be Greek and Jew, circumcision and uncircumcision, barbarian, Scythian, bondman, freeman; but Christ is all, and in all" (Col. 3:10–11). Again, it tells us that natural distinctions no longer exist among believers, for we have become one new man who is created after the image of God. In this new man, all the differences of Greek and Jew, circumcision and uncircumcision, barbarian and Scythian, bondman and freeman have disappeared, for Christ is all and in all.

Having read these three passages of the Bible, we can readily see that all believers are one in Christ. Each and every natural distinction is abrogated. This is a foundational matter for the building up of the church. If we were to bring all these worldly distinctions into the church, we would find that the relationship among brothers and sisters could never be properly adjusted and that the church could not be established before God.

Of the distinctions mentioned in these passages, there are five contrasts, namely, Greek and Jew, bond and free, male and female, barbarian and Scythian, and circumcision and uncircumcision. However, the apostle tells us that in Christ we are one.

The world pays great attention to personal status—to what race do I belong, what background do I have, and so forth. I must maintain my honor; I must protect my status. But once we become Christians, we should exclude all such discriminations. No one should bring his personal status or position into Christ and the church—the one new man; to do so would be to bring in the old man. Nothing that belongs to the old man should ever be carried over into the church.

The Abolishment of National Distinctions

From the viewpoint of the world, national distinctions are the greatest—"Greek and Jew." The Jewish race is listed among those races which have the strongest sense of nationalism. Because they are the descendants of Abraham, chosen by God to be His peculiar people, the only nation established by God, a people that dwell alone and are not reckoned among the nations, they have become very proud of themselves when they ought to humble themselves before God and praise His name. They brag of their being God's people, separated from all the nations. Because of such pride, their nationalism is much stronger than that of many nations. How they despise the Gentiles.

Because of this, it was rather difficult for the Gentiles to be fellow Christians with the Jews. Read the book of Acts and soon you will realize how true the above statement is. On the day of Pentecost the gospel was first preached to the Jews, many of whom accepted the truth of the death and resurrection of the Lord. There was no trouble about preaching to the Jews. Later on in Samaria, many Samaritans, who at least were partially Jewish, were saved through the preaching of the gospel. But for the gospel to be proclaimed among the Gentiles, God had to raise up a special vessel in the person of Paul. Even this did not start abruptly in Antioch, for Peter first started in Caesarea. But being an apostle to the Jews, it was hard to get Peter to go to the Gentiles. God had to give him a vision from heaven thrice, and three times was he charged to rise up, kill, and eat. Without such a vision he would not dare go into the midst of the Gentiles. This was the very first time the gospel was preached to the Gentiles. How reluctant the Jews were to go to the Gentiles with the gospel.

37

Then in Acts 15 the question of circumcision and of keeping the Mosaic law was raised. Some advocated strongly that the Gentiles who had believed in the Lord Jesus should be circumcised and should also keep the law. In other words, they should be Jews as well as Christians; repentance was not only unto being Christians but also unto becoming Jews. How unbreakable was their national concept. Thank God, it was decided in the council at Jerusalem that the Gentiles were not obligated to keep the Mosaic law nor to be circumcised. Paul and Barnabas were free to go to the Gentiles, and thus their fellowship with those in Jerusalem remained intact.

Even after the way for preaching the gospel to the Gentiles was cleared, trouble again arose in Galatians 2 when Peter came to Antioch. At first Peter ate with the Gentiles; but when certain people came from James, he drew back and separated himself, fearing them that were of the circumcision. Paul therefore openly resisted him, for Peter did not walk according to the truth of the gospel. The cross had broken down the middle wall of partition so that now there was neither Jew nor Gentile.

May God graciously open the eyes of young believers to see that no matter whether they were originally Jews or Gentiles, they are now one in Christ. All their national limitations have been broken; national distinctions simply no longer exist. Whether some are American believers, some English believers, some Indian believers, some Japanese believers, or some Chinese believers, they are all brothers and sisters in the Lord. No one can divide them as God's children. We cannot have American Christianity; if we insist on having America, we cannot have Christ. These two are contrary to each other. In Christ, we are all brothers and sisters. It is but natural that no national boundary can exist. The body of Christ is the one new man, completely one, without any national distinctions. Even strong nationalism, such as the Jews had, must be broken in Christ.

Whenever we meet a person in Christ, we should no longer label him as a Chinese or an American, for we are all one in Christ. It is a mistake of the gravest consequence to try to establish a Chinese church or to set up an American testimony. In Christ there is neither Jew nor Gentile. To attempt to bring outside things such as national differences into the church, will completely destroy the things within. In Christ all are coordinated together without any discrimination. The moment distinctions are brought in, the body of Christ is changed into a carnal institution.

Americans are governed by the law of their country. But this national distinction does not apply to our relationship in Christ. Every time we come to the Lord, we come not as Americans or as Chinese but as Christians. We can never approach the Lord on the ground of our nationality. These outside things must be shut out, for we are united by the life of Christ. What we receive is the life of Christ, and this is also what our brethren in England, India and Japan receive. In this life we are united; never on the basis of nationality.

A story we know illustrates this well: after the first world war, some brothers from England went to Germany to attend a conference. One of the brothers in Germany arose to introduce the visitors by saying: "Now that the war is over, we have some English brothers visiting us, to whom we extend our warmest welcome." Among those thus introduced, one stood up and replied: "We are not English brothers, but brothers from England." How well spoken were those words! We cannot have English brothers, American brothers, French sisters, or Italian sisters. We only have brothers from England, America, France or Italy. In Christ there is neither national distinction nor even provincial difference. In the church there is only Christ, for Christ is all in all. Apart from Christ, there is nothing. How glorious this is!

The Elimination of Class Differences

Class relationship is another difficult human relationship. We do not come across national relationships until we meet an alien, but we are confronted with class relationships every day. The apostle mentions that the bond and the free are also eliminated in Christ.

People today may not appreciate the cruelty of class differences. At the time when Paul wrote his letters under the reign of the Roman Empire, the system of slavery was at its worst. There were human markets as well as markets for cattle and for sheep. Many captives of war were sold at the market; children born of slaves were also auctioned in the human exchange. There was a tremendous difference between the free and the bond.

Although the idea of democracy originated in Rome and civil rights, elections, and voting were first practiced there, only freemen could exercise these rights of citizenship; slaves had no such privilege. If a slave were beaten to death, his life was repaid with money to his master, the same as if cattle were killed. Since he had no civil rights, he was not recompensed by a life for a life. This class difference far surpassed the differences today between master and servant, employer and employee, or boss and subordinate. Children born to slaves automatically became slaves and were considered to be the master's property. All slave fugitives could be punished by crucifixion. Yet the Word of God declares that all class differences must be eliminated in Christ.

Suppose Philemon brought Onesimus to the meeting. When they were at home, Onesimus was a servant and Philemon was his master. But when they went to the church, Onesimus was a brother to Philemon, not his servant. The relationship of master and slave does not exist in the church. Even at home when they knelt down to pray, they were brothers; but when they stood up, Onesimus was a slave serving his master, Philemon. So in the new man— that is, in Christ and in the church—all class relationships are nullified. There should not be any consciousness of class difference nor any sense of class struggle.

Assume that you belong to the servant class or that you are an employee or subordinate. In the home or in the office, you should keep your place and learn to listen and obey. But when you and your master or employer or boss come together before God, you do not need to listen to him on the basis of his being your superior. In spiritual matters such class differences do not enter in.

The apostle James condemned strongly the practice of class difference. "For if there come into your synagogue a man with a gold ring, in fine clothing, and there come in also a poor man in vile clothing; and ye have regard to him that weareth the fine clothing, and say, Sit thou here in a good place; and ye say to the poor man, Stand thou there, or sit under my footstool; do ye not make distinctions among yourselves, and become judges with evil thoughts?" (James 2:2–4). As soon as we come to the church and begin to have fellowship with God's children, we must stand on the ground of Christ, of the new man, of the body, and not of class difference.

This elimination of class differences is only possible among Christians. Only Christians can thoroughly carry this out. We Christians can shake one another's hand and declare that we are brothers. We have the love that overcomes differences. In the world, one class tries to overthrow another class, thus raising themselves to a higher class. But we who are in Christ are able to eliminate class discrimination completely. That hard-to-be-broken class difference of freeman and slave must be totally shattered. We fellowship with other brothers and sisters on the sole ground of what the Lord has given to us—His life. Thus shall we receive great blessing from God. Such a church will be full of the love of Christ, and we will be those who minister Christ to one another.

The Exclusion of National Characteristics

The phrase "Jews and Greeks" has in it one more contrast. The Jews represent a highly religious race, while the Greeks stand for philosophy and wisdom. The Jews are historically connected with religion, the Greeks with philosophy. All the basic sciences and philosophies come from the Greeks. Hence scientific terms are usually in Greek. Such are the differences in national characteristics.

To use another illustration: people living in warmer climates are often more warm in temperament while those from colder climates are usually more cool in nature.

Southerners (in the northern hemisphere) are comparatively more emotional and northerners more severe. These are regional characteristics. Let us remember, however, that northerners can be Christians just as well as southerners. Both Jews and Greeks can become Christians. Those who are full of wisdom can be Christians and so can those who are a very religious people. As far as national characteristics go, being religious or being rational are totally different. The scientific knowledge represented by the Greeks stresses the idea of rationalization, whereas religion emphasizes the intuition of the conscience—an entirely different concept.

Nonetheless, in Christ there is no distinction between Jews and Greeks. No one can claim he is a Christian because he is rational and logical about things. Nor can one who follows his conscience exclusively be less Christian than the rational one. According to the flesh, these two persons are totally different. One walks by his huge mind; the other walks by feeling. But there is neither Jew nor Greek in Christ. Not only national differences are abolished; even national characteristics are excluded. One may be a Christian with a cool and severe attitude or he may be one in a warm and emotional way. The one who depends on rationalization can be a Christian; so can the other who lives by inward feeling. All kinds of people can be Christians.

Yet, when anyone becomes a Christian, he must leave his national characteristics outside the church for there is no such thing in the church. Today there are problems in many churches caused by the intrusion of national peculiarities. Those who are talkative group together; so do those who dislike talking. The cool gather together and the warm do likewise. Thus there exist many differences among God's children.

Please remember: national characteristics have no place in the church, in the new man, in Christ. Do not judge others because they have a different temperament. They will judge you in the same way if you do. You may wonder why they are so cold when you talk to them so warmly. Perhaps, though, they are suffering at the same time with your peculiarity.

A new believer therefore must learn to let his temperament remain outside the door of the church, for it does not belong inside. Otherwise he will create lots of unnecessary criticism. All those natural things which he brings in will in turn become the source of criticism, confusion and division. He will divide the brethren. He will set himself up as the standard. All who meet his standards are good Christians, whereas the rest are not. As he brings in his temperament and his characteristics, he also brings confusion to the church. Neither his coolness nor his warmth is good; neither his rationalization nor his feeling is good—all these are differences which exist outside of Christ, differences represented by the Jews and the Greeks. None should be brought into the church.

Many who come into the church affirm that they are such-and-such naturally. They say it rather proudly. But they should be told that the church does not need their natural selves. They ought not to bring their old selves to the church, for it is not in Christ and it tends to divide.

Consequently, we must reject everything that belongs to the old man. Only thus can we go on with all the children of God.

The Dismissal of Cultural Divergences

There is a contrast in Colossians 3:11, that of barbarian and Scythian, which puzzles commentators. A barbarian is a man in a rude, uncivilized state; sometimes specifically one in a state between savagery and civilization (Webster). But what a Scythian is, is a mystery. Some consider him as more barbarous than the barbarian, for the savageness of the Scythians is proverbial (J. B. Lightfoot); while others, such as B. F. Westcott, reflect that since in the classics the Scythians are often mentioned together with the Galatians, they must be a very respectable people.* Whatever interpretation we may personally accept, the point is that certain places are known for their specific qualities. The people of Foochow† are famed for their inability to do business and for claiming bankruptcy, the people of Shansi (a province in northwest China) are noted for their ability in money dealings and for the high interest rate they get, and the people of Shaohsing (a city in Chekiang province) are known as counsellors and attorneys. Each place is associated with a singular quality.

From the standpoint of culture, some are to be respected and some are to be despised. In the world this distinction is quite sharp. We cannot put a typical English gentleman together with an African savage. This is not a question of class difference but a matter of cultural disparity. The Englishman may be an employee, a domestic servant, or a cook, while the African savage may be a king or a tribal head. The class difference is thus that of an employee contrasted with a king; culturally, though, they fare quite dif-

---

* Editor's note: brother Nee takes the latter view.
† Editor's note: a city in south China, native place of brother Watchman Nee.

ferently. Each may look down on the other with some reason. However, Paul tells us that the distinction between barbarian and Scythian is annulled.

Once I met two Jews with whom I became quite familiar. So I asked them candidly why were the Jews opposed by so many people in the world. One of them answered, "It is because our Jewish culture is inferior to others." Not knowing exactly his meaning, I further asked him to explain. Now this friend had quite a high social standing. He said, "I am an American Jew. As an American I honestly hate the Jews because our Jewish culture is too crude." This, in fact, illustrates how the Scythians despise the barbarians. My friend continued, "Suppose an American earns two hundred dollars per month. After paying for his rent and food, he can live comfortably on what is left.* He has the habit of polishing his shoes and changing his shirt daily. He may still save ten dollars or more each month. But a person who is a Jew would spend only ten dollars and save one hundred and ninety dollars. The American uses one hundred ninety dollars and keeps only ten dollars, but the Jew thinks in terms of money saved rather than of cultural achievement. He figures how he can save money by not polishing his shoes or changing his shirt daily. He prefers to live in a smaller place so long as his bank account rises. The Jews despise the Americans because the latter are so poor; the Americans disdain the Jews because they live so poorly and dress so carelessly. Culturally these two people are different; hence all the problems." Then he concluded with the remark, "We Jews have money and

---

* Editor's note: let the reader remember that these messages were spoken in 1948.

good brains, but we lack in culture. Therefore we do not mix well with other people and as a result we are not welcome." This was the first time I ever heard such a thing said in this way.

It is, indeed, most difficult for the culturally high to mix with the culturally low. This is not a matter of class or of wisdom or wealth but totally a question of culture. The lack of culture breeds contempt. From the viewpoint of the Scythian, a barbarian is wanting in everything—not knowing how to dress, how to eat, and how to live. But from the eyes of the barbarian, the Scythians are just too materialistic, paying too much attention to eating and dressing. Their viewpoints are so opposite that there is bound to be conflict if both are taken into the church. How can the barbarian and the Scythian be reconciled to each other if both have such strong opinions?

Suppose one eats with chopsticks while the other uses his hands. When they dine together, the former feels uncomfortable though he restrains himself from saying anything at first. He looks upon the latter as uncivilized. After two days his endurance may reach its limit and so he begins to pick on the latter. In the meantime, he who eats with hands may have the same trouble with the one who eats with chopsticks. He cannot understand why people do not eat naturally but must eat in such an artificial manner. The difference, therefore, is great. Neither can claim he is absolutely right. Such is cultural divergence, a thing of the world, without any foundation in the Lord.

As a matter of fact, cultural divergence does cause lots of trouble, but we must remember that this too has been deleted in Christ. We who are in Christ are big men and women. We alone can endure what the world cannot

47

stand. We make no distinction among brethren. We do not set ourselves up as being the standard and judge everyone accordingly. Such a situation simply does not exist in Christ, in the church, in the one new man. Some brothers may come from India, some from Africa. Their cultures are greatly different from ours, but we ask only one question: are they in the Lord? They too ask only the same question concerning us. If all are in the Lord, everything is settled. We maintain our contact in the Lord; we love one another in the Lord. We can endure everything else and refuse to allow anything to divide us as children of God.

Could we gather all the sophisticated brethren and form a church with them? Or gather all the simple brethren and form another church? No, neither of these would be the church. It is true that the conflict of culture is a very hard matter to endure. Yet it is equally true that this cultural divergence does not belong in the church. It is something outside the body of Christ. Never bring it into the church. Never allow it to become an issue.

On the other hand, we should each one of us be as a Roman when we are among the Romans; as one under the law to them that are under the law (see 1 Cor. 9:20–22). We should learn to be under the same culture as the people among whom we live. If some brothers come to China from Africa, they should learn how to use chopsticks. If some of us go to Africa, we too should adapt ourselves to eating with our hands. We do not want to be different from the local brethren. We learn their customs if we happen to visit Africa; they learn ours if they come to visit us. Among the English, let us be as Englishmen; among the Chinese, as Chinese. Wherever we go, we become one with the local people. Otherwise, we will hurt their feelings; we will not be able to gain them. Should the Lord give us opportunity for contact with people of a different culture, we must learn to adapt ourselves. In Christ, we are one; therefore, we stand on this ground of oneness with all God's children.

No Show of Piety in the Flesh

Another contrast is "circumcision and uncircumcision." This speaks of the distinctions in outward signs of piety in the flesh. We all know that Jews receive circumcision in their flesh. They have the sign upon them. They profess that they belong to God, that they are God-fearing, and that they deny the flesh. By this sign in the flesh, they are confident of having part in God's covenant.

The Jews lay much stress on circumcision. This is a characteristic of Judaism. He who is circumcised is included in the covenant of God; he who is uncircumcised is excluded from God's covenant. No one is allowed to marry the uncircumcised. In Acts 15, circumcision was the focus of discussion, for some of the Jewish believers would have liked to force circumcision on the Gentiles. The whole book of Galatians deals with this matter of circumcision. Paul declares that if he were to preach circumcision, the salvation of the cross would no longer exist, for people would simply depend on an outward show of piety in the flesh.

To enlarge on this in its application: I was baptized by immersion but a certain brother was sprinkled. The Word of God shows that believers should be immersed. I consider myself as having the sign of piety in my flesh. The other brother lacks this sign. So I judge him as being inadequate. Thus I make immersion a cause of distinction. (I must add, however, that we do not suggest immersion is unnecessary.)

Another illustration is the matter of head-covering for the sisters, something spiritual in meaning but physical in symbol. Or consider the breaking of bread and the laying on of hands, both of which are rich in spiritual significance yet not without physical expression. All of these are spiritual things, but if we use these to divide God's children, then we downgrade them from spiritual realities into fleshly signs. They belong to the same category as circumcision.

Let us understand, not misunderstand, our meaning here. We do not say that baptism, breaking of bread, head-covering, and laying on of hands are not necessary. What we do say is that no one should divide God's children with these things, for in so doing he relegates them to the flesh—and the flesh always divides. In Christ there is neither circumcision nor uncircumcision. No sign in the flesh may be used to differentiate the children of God. We are one in Christ for we share one life. These outward things are practiced only because they have corresponding spiritual realities. If any should have the reality but lack the outward sign, he should not for this reason be separated from the other children of God. No sign in the flesh should affect our oneness in Christ. The value of the spiritual reality of our oneness far exceeds the value of the outward sign.

Paul makes it quite clear that circumcision does not take away the defilement of the flesh, for it is only aimed at curtailing the activities of the flesh. What is important is the inward, not the outward things. If the inward vision is the same, though the outward expression may be slightly different, no division would be made. In case there is neither the inward reality nor the outward sign, then the responsibility is on that person, not on us.

The Suspension of Sex Disparity

The last distinction to be suspended in Christ is the matter of sex. In church government, male and female have their respective positions. When the church meets, the man functions differently from the woman. In the family, husband and wife hold different responsibilities. But *in Christ,* there can be no male and female. Neither the man nor the woman has any peculiar position. Why? Because Christ is all and is in all. Notice the word "all" used twice. Christ is both all and in all. Hence, in spiritual life there is absolutely no way to differentiate between male and female.

No doubt in the realm of service, the sisters sometimes have a different ministry from that of the brothers. This is due to the arrangement in the order of authority of this present age; but when we come to the future age, the arrangement will be different. However, even today, there can be no difference in Christ. Both the brother and the sister are saved by the life of the Son of God. Both become children of God. The word "children" (Greek "teknon") makes no distinction between male or female (though according to its root it is masculine in form).

How, then, are we going to explain 2 Corinthians 6:17–18? "Wherefore come ye out from among them, and be ye separate, saith the Lord, and touch no unclean thing; and I will receive you, and will be to you a Father, and ye shall be to me sons and daughters, saith the Lord Almighty." Take note: the Word does not suggest that due to our leaving the world we will be born again; instead, it states that having believed in God we should come out of the world and be separated from the unclean so that God the Father may receive us as receiving His sons and daughters. It does not deal with the basic matter of our being in Christ or with our primary relationship with God; it touches rather upon our being accepted as His beloved sons and daughters. It is very personal in approach; that is, if any should suffer loss for the sake of God, he will find in his distress that God is his Father and he is a son to God. Whether one is male or female makes no difference, for God will accept him as son and her as daughter. So long as one is accepted by God what does it matter? He is the All-Sufficient God who possesses all things. In forsaking the world, one is met by God. Herein we have sons and daughters because this refers to personal relationship, not to that basic relationship in Christ. In Christ, we are all God's children. Sex disparity simply does not exist in Christ.

In Shanghai there was a brother who was a carpenter. Once I asked him, "Brother, what is the spiritual condition of the brothers in your place?" He answered, "Are you asking about the male brothers or the female brothers?" I considered that an excellent expression. He did not know whether I meant the brothers or the sisters. The male brothers are brothers, the female brothers are brothers too. In Christ there is no disparity. How true was his answer for in simplicity he had uttered the truth of the Scripture. Therefore let new believers take to heart that when we come to Christ, we have transcended the relationship of male and female. The disparity of sex is suspended in Christ.

We are all brothers and sisters. We are each a new creation in Christ. We are members of the one body. All natural distinctions have been annulled in Christ. We therefore must shut out of our hearts any party spirit, any divisive spirit. So shall we advance one step further.

WITNESSING

The Testimony of the Church

A candle that stands alone can easily be blown out by the wind. Even if it is not extinguished by the wind, its light will eventually burn out. If we want to increase and prolong the light, we need to kindle more candles and to continue to do so. Suppose we kindle ten candles, one hundred candles, or even one thousand candles; then the light will continue on. And this is the way it is with the testimony of the church.

It is pitiful that light and testimony cease with some individuals. Whereas the church ought to propagate herself from generation to generation, there are a number of people who have no descendants. May it not be that the testimony of Jesus terminates in some new believers. A candle should burn until it is all burned; likewise, a man's testimony should continue until his death. If the light of a candle is to be continued, then the candle needs to kindle another candle before it is completely burned. By kindling candle after candle, the light will shine on and on until it covers the whole world. Such is the testimony of the church.

New believers must learn to witness for the Lord; otherwise the gospel will terminate with them. You are already saved; you have life and your light is kindled. But if you do not ignite others before you are all burned up, then you are really finished. You should bring many to the Lord lest you see Him empty-handed.

I have said before that if a believer does not open his mouth and confess the Lord within the first year of his salvation, he probably will never open his mouth all through his life. Today I want to repeat this. If a man does not witness for the Lord during the first flush of his faith, he probably will never witness throughout his life. Unless the Lord grants him great grace or gives him a mighty revival, he most likely will never bear witness for the Lord and bring souls to Christ. What hope is there with young believers if they cannot witness for the Lord and ignite other people when for the first time they receive so great a love, so great a Lord, so great a salvation, and so great an emancipation?

If a new believer does not open his mouth during the first year, he will hardly be able to open his mouth later on. That is why it is our responsibility to instruct each and every new believer to start witnessing during the first or second week of his salvation. We must be firm in this matter. It may be too late if we wait.

Let us continue with the illustration of the candle. When the Son of God came to the earth, He kindled a few candles; later He ignited another candle in Paul. During the two thousand years since then, the church has continued burning on and on with candle after candle. Some candles may ignite tens or hundreds of candles. Though the first candle burns out, the second one continues. Many may even sacrifice their lives to ignite you; we do not expect to see the light terminate in you. We expect all new believers to fulfill their duty of saving souls. Go and witness for the Lord. Bring souls to Christ. Let the testimony shine on the earth unceasingly.

The Meaning of Witnessing

There are a number of Scripture verses quoted in the following pages which we would especially like to consider. The first group of two passages will tell us what it means to witness for the Lord.

"For thou shalt be a witness for him unto all men of what thou hast seen and heard" (Acts 22:15). The Lord spoke these words to Paul through Ananias. Whatever you have seen and heard, you shall witness to all men. So the first foundation of witnessing is seeing and hearing. You cannot testify what you have not seen or heard. The advantage Paul had was that unlike other people he personally had heard and seen the Lord. He witnessed to that which he had seen and heard.

"And we have beheld and bear witness that the Father hath sent the Son to be the Saviour of the world" (1 John 4:14). This tells us what witnessing is. We witness to what we have seen. Thank God, you have recently believed in the Lord. You have met Him, believed in Him, and received Him. You are now redeemed. Having been set free from sin and having received forgiveness, you have peace in you. You know how happy you are after you have believed—a happiness which you never knew before.

Formerly the load of sin weighed heavily upon you, but today, thank God, this load has rolled away. So you are a person who has seen and heard. What should you do now? You should send forth your testimony. This does not mean you are to be a preacher or to leave your job and be a full-time worker. It only means you are to witness to your friends and relatives and acquaintances of that which you have seen and heard. You should try to bring souls to the Lord.

How to Witness

The above two Scripture passages form a set on the meaning of witnessing. Now we will turn to another set, a set of four passages which will tell us very simply what witnessing is.

1. Speak in the City—The Samaritan Woman

In John 4 the Samaritan woman met the Lord who then asked her for water. But after asking, the Lord turned around and offered her the living water without which no one could really live and be satisfied. He who drinks of the water of the well will thirst again. There will at least be as many times of thirstiness as there are times of drinking. You will never be satisfied, so you have to drink again and again. What the world can offer may satisfy for a time but sooner or later thirstiness will return. Only the fountain that springs up from within can satisfy forever. This inward satisfaction alone can deliver people from the demand of the world.

After the Lord Jesus showed the Samaritan woman who He was, the woman left her waterpot—until then something most important to her—and went into the city and said, "Come, see a man, who told me all things that ever I did; can this be the Christ?" (v. 29). Here we have a real example of witnessing.

This woman had been married five times, but she was still unsatisfied. It was like drinking water; she had to drink again and again. But on that day the Lord told her that He had living water which really satisfied. No wonder after she came to know such a great Savior, she threw away her waterpot and testified in the city. Her first act was to witness for Christ.

What did she testify? She said, "Here is a man who told me everything that I ever did" (see v. 39). She had done lots of things; some known to the public but some unknown. She was afraid to tell people all that she had done; yet now the Lord had done just that. So she testified that here was a man who told everything that she ever had done, things which she herself alone knew. Could this man be the Christ? Let me tell you: as soon as she saw the Lord, she opened her mouth. The Bible says, "And from that city many of the Samaritans believed on him because of the word of the woman, who testified" (v. 39).

From this we may see one thing: everyone has the need to testify, to tell his own story. Since the Lord has saved such a big sinner as you, can you shut your mouth and not testify? The Savior has saved me; I cannot but open my mouth and confess Him. Though I cannot explain why, at least I see that this is God, this is Christ, this is God's Son, this is God's appointed Savior. I can also see that I am a sinner saved by grace. All that is required of me is to express my feeling. I may not be able to tell what has happened, but you all can see how greatly I am changed. I do not know how it happened—I, who formerly considered myself a good man, today see myself as a sinner. What I did not regard as sin, the Lord has pointed out to me to be sinful. Now I know what sort of a person I am. I did many things in the past without anyone's knowledge; sometimes even I myself was not aware of what I did. I sinned greatly but I was not conscious of being sinful. Yet here came a Man who told me all things that I ever did. He told me that which I did not know as well as that which I did know. I have to confess that I have touched the Savior. This One must be Christ who alone can save.

Whoever has seen himself a sinner surely has a testimony to give. He who has seen the Savior is a good witness. Remember, this Samaritan woman gave her testimony within an hour after she had met the Lord. She did it on the first day. She did not wait a few years until she came back from a revival meeting. No; as soon as she returned home, she immediately witnessed for the Lord.

It is right for a person soon after he is saved to tell others what he has seen and understood. There is no need to give a long discourse; just telling what you know is quite sufficient. One person might say, "Before I believed in the Lord I could not sleep at night, but now I am able to sleep. I used to be depressed, but now I feel good no matter what happens to me." Another might say, "Formerly I could not eat, but now I can eat." All you need to do is tell the fact. You need not talk about what you do not know.

Brothers and sisters should learn not to say too much. Do not talk beyond your comprehension, lest you stir up arguments. Set yourselves as living witnesses among men of what you have experienced; against this no one can argue.

2. Witness at Home—the Demoniac

In Mark 5:1-20, we find a man who was terribly possessed by an unclean spirit. He cut himself with stones, and no man had strength to tame him. He rent the chains that bound him, and broke the fetters in pieces. He dwelt in the tombs, and people dared not pass that place. But the Lord cast the unclean spirit out of that man. He wanted to follow the Lord, but the Lord bade him, "Go to thy house unto thy friends, and tell them how great things the Lord hath done for thee, and how he had mercy on thee" (v. 19). To tell what great things the Lord has done for you is witnessing for the Lord.

This demoniac could not live in a house but only dwelt in tombs. A tomb is a place for the dead, so this living person dwelt in the place for the dead. When the Lord commanded the unclean spirits to depart from that man, those unclean spirits "entered into the swine: and the herd rushed down the steep into the sea, in number about two thousand; and they were drowned in the sea" (v. 13). What that man endured of the demoniac power was unendurable to the two thousand swine. No wonder he cut himself with stones, for who can fall into the hands of demons and not cut himself! In the case of the Samaritan woman we see a person who sought the pleasures of the world, but in this case we witness a fierce person. The Lord saved him and sent him home to tell his relatives what great things the Lord had done for him and what mercy the Lord had shown him.

When you receive grace, you ought to let your family, your neighbors, and your relatives know that you are now a saved person. Tell them what great things the Lord has done for you as well as how you have believed in Him. Tell them the fact and truthfully witness to them. Thus you will ignite other people and let the salvation of the Lord continue on.

3. PROCLAIM IN THE SYNAGOGUES—SAUL

"And he was certain days with the disciples that were at Damascus. And straightway in the synagogues he proclaimed Jesus, that he is the Son of God. And all that heard him were amazed, and said, Is not this he that in Jerusalem made havoc of them that called on this name? and he had come hither for this intent, that he might bring them bound before the chief priests" (Acts 9:19b–21). The word "straightway" is quite emphatic in the Greek.

The apostle John tells us that whoever believes Jesus to be the Son of God is begotten of God. Saul was instantaneously saved after he met the light. But when he was brought to the city of Damascus, his eyes could not see and he was very weak physically. After he was baptized by Ananias, he took food and was strengthened. A few days later he straightway proclaimed in the synagogues that Jesus is the Son of God. There was a very definite problem involved in Saul's taking this step, for he was one of the members of the Sanhedrin. The Jewish Sanhedrin was composed of seventy members and he was one of them. He had taken with him from Jerusalem letters from the chief priest to bind all those who believed on the Lord Jesus and to send them to the chief priest. Now that he himself had accepted the Lord Jesus, what ought he to do? Formerly he came to bind those who accepted the Lord; now he himself was subject to being bound. But instead of fleeing for his life, he entered the synagogues and proved to the people that Jesus is the Son of God.

So the first thing a person should do after receiving the Lord is to witness for the Lord. As soon as Saul's eyes were healed, he seized the first opportunity to testify that Jesus is the Son of God. Let me tell you: each and everyone who believes in the Lord Jesus should do just that.

Most unbelievers who have heard of the name of Jesus or have read about Him in history consider Him as Jesus of Nazareth. The world acknowledges that there was a Jesus, but that He was only one more among the billions. In other words, in their eyes Jesus was only one man among many; though He may have been comparatively special, yet he was still an ordinary person. Wait until one day, though, when the unbeliever receives light and the eyes of his heart are opened. Then he gets a revelation; then he discovers the fact that Jesus is the Son of God. He may well rush to his friend's home even if it is after midnight to tell him that he has found God's Son and His name is Jesus.

It is a tremendous thing to find among men One who is the Son of God. This is a monumental discovery. It surely should not be taken lightly. Out of the thousands of years of history and the billions of people who have lived, you have found One who is the Son of God. Is this a small thing?

Here was a man, Paul, traveling on an animal's back and plotting the death of all who believed in the name of Jesus. But after he got up from falling off the animal, he entered into the synagogues and proclaimed that Jesus is the Son of God. Let me tell you: unless Paul had been out of his mind, he must have seen a vision. He must have received a revelation. Out of the billions of people who have lived on this earth he picked One whom he proclaimed to be the Son of God. New believers also should be like Paul and go out and proclaim that they have met God's Son.

Can a person get saved and sit quietly as if nothing has happened? Can he believe on the Lord Jesus and not feel amazingly surprised? I doubt that anyone can do that, for he has made a tremendous discovery, the most special of all: Jesus of Nazareth is the Son of God! I would not at all be surprised if he knocked on the door of his friend's house after midnight. Indeed, he ought to climb to the mountaintop to shout the news or go to the seashore to proclaim that Jesus of Nazareth is the Son of God! No other discovery is anywhere near the magnitude of this one. Even putting all the world's discoveries together would fall far behind this one. Indeed, we have discovered the Son of God. What a tremendous thing this is!

Suppose a governor, a chairman, a president, a marshall, or a king travels incognito, but you recognize him because you have such a keen eye. You feel elated for you have made a great discovery. The Son of God also travels incognito, but we have discovered Him. Jesus of Nazareth is the Son of God. This is a tremendous thing. For this reason, when Peter confessed the Lord as the Son of the living God the Lord Jesus said to him, "For flesh and blood hath not revealed it unto thee, but my Father who is in heaven" (Matt. 16:17b). When He travels incognito, He is known by no one except those to whom the Father reveals Him.

Therefore, new believers, never consider your faith as a small thing. Why does Christianity emphasize faith? Because it surpasses anything the world has. You have believed. What a wonderful thing is the faith which you have. You can shout and proclaim everywhere—on the streets, in the synagogue, or in meeting places, that you have found out that Jesus of Nazareth is the Son of God. Your brother, Paul, did just that. If you too realize what it is you have found, you will do the same thing. Jesus of Nazareth is the Son of God. What a wonderful and most glorious fact it is.

4. PERSONAL WITNESSING

One of the two that heard John speak, and followed him, was Andrew, Simon Peter's brother. He findeth first his own brother Simon, and saith unto him, We have found the Messiah (which is, being interpreted, Christ). He brought him unto Jesus. Jesus looked upon him, and said, Thou art Simon the son of John: thou shalt be called Cephas (which is by interpretation, Peter).

On the morrow he was minded to go forth into Galilee, and he findeth Philip: and Jesus saith unto him, Follow me. Now Philip was from Bethsaida, of the city of Andrew and Peter. Philip findeth Nathanael, and saith unto him, We have found him, of whom Moses in the law, and the prophets, wrote, Jesus of Nazareth, the son of Joseph.

John 1:40–45

In this fourth passage, we find how Andrew sought out Simon, and Philip sought out Nathaniel. From this we learn that after we believe in the Lord we should not only witness in the city, at home, and in the synagogues but also should witness person to person.

As soon as Andrew believed in the Lord, he led his brother Peter to Christ. Later on it turned out that Peter possessed more gifts and probably was a greater apostle. Yet it was Andrew who led Peter to the Lord. First he was saved and then he brought in his brother. The relationship between Philip and Nathaniel was not that of brothers but of friends. Philip sought out his friend and brought the latter to the Lord. Both these examples illustrate the principle of personal witnessing.

Let us remember that the foundation of Christianity is built on this one-by-one method. About a hundred years ago, there was a believer in England by the name of Harvey Page. His eyes were opened by the special grace of the Lord to see that, though he was a most simple person having no conspicuous gift and unable to do many things, yet he could at least deal with people one by one. Though many Christians were gifted to do great works, he was not. But he could focus his attention on one person and follow through with that one person tenaciously. Thus he would tell his chosen friend that since he, Harvey Page, was saved, his friend could be saved too. He would pray for and talk to his friend until the latter did indeed get saved. By the time Harvey Page departed from this world, he had in this manner led more than a hundred people to the Lord.

Succeeding Harvey Page was Thomas Hogban and his One-by-One Band. Hogban was actually touched by Page's faithfulness. He was a learned man and a man of prayer. He organized the One-by-One Band in twenty-seven countries. Though this work has now been terminated, during the time of its existence many were saved.

A new believer may feel that he is not much gifted, but like Andrew and Philip he should at once witness to his family or to his friends. If his strength is limited, he can at least focus on one person at a time. Thus shall he bring souls to the Lord.

When to Witness

One ought to bear witness as soon as he believes on the Lord. Whether he witnesses to one or to many, in his home or in the city, in the early morning or at midday, in one place or in many places, in the synagogues or in the villages, he must bear witness for the Lord.

It is a great blessing if one can start to save souls on the first day of his salvation. I remember a story about a battalion commander. Mr. Todd was a great soul-winner in the last century. He was saved when he was sixteen and this is what then happened: On a certain holiday he went to a village where he was entertained by a couple in the church. This couple was wise in soul-winning, and they brought Todd to the Lord. Todd had formerly been a carefree youth, but on that day he knelt down to pray and was saved. Afterwards he had tea with the couple. During their conversation, he was told that the gospel could not become strong in that locality until a certain battalion commander was converted.*

Young Todd asked who this Commander Deeds was. He was told that the man was a retired commander of over sixty years of age who looked on all Christians as hypocrites and who would curse or beat any Christian who dared to preach the gospel to him or even to pass by his house. He kept a pistol at home and threatened to open fire on any who preached to him. Having heard this, Todd immediately prayed: "O Lord, You have shown grace to me. This is the first day of my salvation. I will go and witness to him." Before tea was finished, he was on his way to

* Translator's note: we cannot check on the correct name of the commander, so we tentatively call him Deeds.

the commander. It was less than two hours after he was saved.

The elderly couple tried to advise Todd not to go. It would be futile since many had already witnessed to the commander without success. Some of these he had beaten with the end of his pistol or with a rod; some he had threatened to shoot. Nobody would sue him for being beaten for the sake of the gospel since that would be against our Lord's teaching. As a result, the commander became fiercer and fiercer. But Todd still felt he should go.

He arrived at the house and knocked on the door. The commander answered the door with a rod in his hand and said, "Young man, what do you want?" Todd requested to have a few words with him. So they both entered into the room. "I hope you will accept the Lord Jesus as your Savior," said Todd. The commander lifted up his rod, saying, "I suppose you are new here so I pardon you; I will not beat you. Have you not heard that this is one place where the name of Jesus is tabooed? Now, go quickly!"

"I beg you to believe on the Lord Jesus," continued Todd. The commander was furious. He went upstairs and came down with his pistol. "Go, or I will shoot," he threatened. Todd answered, "I have come to ask you to believe in the Lord Jesus. If you want to shoot, you may. But before you shoot, let me pray." He immediately knelt before the commander and prayed: "O God, here is a man who does not know You. Please save him." He prayed the second time: "O God, here is a man who does not know You. Have mercy on him, have mercy on the commander." He kept on kneeling and praying, "O God, have mercy on the commander." After he had prayed five or six times, he heard a sigh and then heard the pistol being laid aside.

After a while, the commander also knelt down by the side of Todd and then he too prayed, saying, "O God, have mercy on Commander Deeds." Within five minutes the commander was saved. As they rose he took the hand of the young man and said, "I have *heard* the gospel all my life, but today I have *seen* the gospel for the first time." Young Todd later told people that when he saw those fierce-looking lines on the sin-stained face of the commander, it seemed as if light shone through every one of them pleading for the mercy of God. On the following Lord's day, Commander Deeds went to the church to worship. And before he died he led several dozen people to the Lord.

The Believer's Secret of Happiness

In every believer's life there are two big days, two days of special rejoicing. The first happy day is the day when he believes in the Lord. The second happy day is the day when he for the first time leads someone to Christ. To many, the joy of leading a person to the Lord for the very first time even exceeds the joy of their own salvation. But many believers are not happy, for they have never uttered a word for the Lord nor ever led a soul to Christ. Do not let this be your condition; do not degenerate to the point of having no joy.

The Bible says, "And he that is wise winneth souls" (Prov. 11:30b). New believers should learn to bring souls to salvation from the start of their Christian life. They must learn to be wise so as to be useful in the church of God. The spiritual understanding of many believers has never been opened because they do not know how to win souls. We do not encourage people to preach in the pulpit, but we do persuade them to save souls. Many can preach but cannot save souls. If you bring people to them, they do not know how to deal with these souls. Only those who know how to deal with souls and lead them to Christ are useful in the church. May new believers learn this early in their Christian life.

It is absolutely impossible for a person to have light and not to shine. As there is no tooth which does not chew, no fountain that does not flow, so there is no life which does not beget life. Whoever cannot witness to sinners is probably in need of others testifying to him. Whoever has no interest to help people repent and believe in the Lord may himself need to repent and believe the Lord. Whoever is voiceless for the Lord may have yet to hear the sound of God's gospel. Is there any light without a ray or a fountain without water? Is it possible for a man to be so advanced spiritually that he is no longer winning souls? I am not talking about preaching but about saving souls. I am not talking about giving a gospel message but about witnessing. Who can be so spiritually progressed as to have no need to witness to people? Therefore new believers ought to learn to bear witness for the Lord. This is something you can never outgrow; it is a lifetime undertaking.

When you are a little further along the road of spiritual growth, some brothers may say to you that you should be a channel of living water. Indeed, we do need to be joined to the Holy Spirit so that living water may flow through us. But let me also say that the channel of life has two ends: one end is opened towards the Holy Spirit, towards the Lord, towards life; but the other end is opened towards men. If the end towards men is shut, living water will never be able to flow out. How can anyone be so misled as to think that having one end opened towards the Lord is adequate? No, the water of life will not flow if only the end towards the Lord is opened. The other end, the end towards men, towards the world, towards sinners must be opened too in order for there to be any flowing. The reason why many do not have power before God is due to their either being closed on the end towards the Lord or on the end towards sinners.

Today I would like to make some calculations, even as others before me have done. Should there be ten thousand believers who hereafter faithfully bear witness everywhere with one accord, they should be able to save the whole world population within ten years if each of them leads three persons to the Lord yearly.* This is not something that will be done from the pulpit, but rather through personal witnessing. From this computation, we may realize how very lazy we are in saving souls. How great is the loss!

The Duty of Witnessing

Because you are not witnessing, many have not heard the gospel. They will be eternally separated, not just temporarily separated, from God. What a consequence!

Dr. Chalmers was one of the best preachers and soul-winners during the second half of the last century. The following story comes from him: Once he was invited to have supper in a family. After they had finished eating, they read the Bible. Being a most learned and eloquent man, Dr. Chalmers talked with the others a great deal on

---

* Based on population estimates of 1948 or earlier.

learned matters. At that time two very elderly tribal chieftains were present, one of whom was also a very learned man. So they talked for a long time. Later they all retired to their rooms. This learned chieftain happened to occupy a room opposite to Dr. Chalmers'. As Dr. Chalmers retired to his room, he heard a sound like something falling in the opposite room. He ran over and discovered the chieftain dead on the floor. The others in the house also rushed over to the room.

Immediately Dr. Chalmers stood up and said: "Had I known that this would happen, I would not have spent the last two hours chatting about so many things. I would have pointed him to eternal things. But, alas, I have not used even five minutes to speak to him of the salvation of his soul. I did not even give him a chance. If I had known then what I know now, I would have used all my strength to tell him how Jesus was crucified on the cross for him. But now it is too late. Had I spoken those words to him at that time, you all might have laughed at me and considered my conversation as inappropriate. Though I now say these words, the time is too late. At supper I could have said them, words which now I hope you all will listen to. Each and every one of you needs the Lord Jesus and His cross. Let me tell you, separation from God is eternal, not temporary. How sad that this man is eternally barred from heaven."

New believers must not be lax in this matter. We must learn to bring people to the Lord. We need to have a determination within us to win souls. Let us at least let them hear the gospel of Jesus Christ. When I was newly saved, I was told by those older in the Lord that I should at least speak to one soul a day. Unless the new believer is a sick person confined at home, we encourage all to speak of the Lord Jesus to at least one person a day.

It is best that you keep a record of how many souls you have won to Christ—thirty, forty, or fifty a year. We are afraid of general prayers asking the Lord to save souls. You should set a goal for the year: ten, twenty, or thirty. You should pray: "Lord, I ask You for thirty souls." Record in your book the name of each who is saved. At the close of the year, check your book and if it does not balance with your prayer ask the Lord for the deficit. Do encourage brothers and sisters to do this. Let me tell you: it is not too much to save thirty, forty, or fifty people. It should be very common to ask for ten or twenty. You need to have a definite number to ask the Lord for fulfillment. Pray daily before the Lord and seize every opportunity to witness for Christ.

At least witness to one person a day. Witness to whomever you meet. It is useless for the gospel to be preached only from the pulpit. Young people ought to learn to witness daily, to seize opportunity daily to work for the Lord. Do not conceive a fanciful expectation of ascending the pulpit without having any sense of daily duty in personal witnessing. It is futile. We expect all young people to be engaged in personal work, in speaking one to one.

D. L. Moody was a great soul-winner. He had a rule: whether in the pulpit or not, we must preach the gospel to at least one person each day. One night he went to bed and suddenly remembered that he had not preached the gospel that day. What should he do? He got up and dressed. It was already midnight and there was nobody on the street. He could do nothing but try to find a policeman. He exhorted the policeman to believe in the Lord. It happened that the policeman he talked to was in great distress, so Moody was rebuffed by the policeman angrily, saying, "What sort of a person are you to do nothing but to persuade me to believe in Jesus at midnight?" Moody spoke a few more words and then hurried home. But, thank God, after a few days the policeman was saved.

I hope all able-bodied new believers will determine before God that they will seize every opportunity to find souls and to find at least one soul per day. If the whole church is preaching the gospel, who can stand against it?

May we lift up our torches and ignite others. May the testimony of the gospel be continued in us until the Lord shall come. Let not the testimony cease when our candles are burned out. May this candle of ours kindle another candle and still another candle. It is not too much to ask for thirty, forty, or fifty people a year from the Lord. Yearly let us bring souls to Christ. Thus shall the church be prosperous. There is much work before us. Let us all rise up and finish the task.

HOW TO LEAD PEOPLE TO CHRIST

We have already mentioned to new believers the importance of witnessing. Now we will instruct them on *how* to lead people to the Lord. The lack of such knowledge will no doubt render much of their witnessing ineffective. After a person is saved, he must not only be exhorted to go out and witness but he also needs to be instructed on how to lead men to Christ. These two things he needs to learn and to do.

Let us look at the matter of how to lead people to the Lord from two sides: first, approaching God on behalf of sinners; and second, approaching sinners on behalf of God and the technique of how to lead people to the Lord.

Approach God on Behalf of Sinners

1. PREPARE A RECORD BOOK

The first thing to do is to prepare a notebook. Ask God to give the names of those whom He wishes to save into your heart. No doubt you will be burdened in your heart to pray for a few or even for several dozen people.

Do not compile this name list carelessly, for that would be a waste of time. The important thing is that before you write down the names, you first ask the Lord to put them into your heart. For the work to be done well, it must begin well. As you lay this matter before the Lord, He will give you the names of certain ones for whom to pray. The names of your family, your friends, your colleagues, your schoolmates, and your acquaintances will spontaneously come to your heart. You hope that these people will soon be saved.

Enter these names in the record book according to the number of their occurrence. Under a date column write the date you started to pray for a certain person, and over on the other side keep a blank to be filled in with the time when that particular person is saved. Once a name is entered, it cannot be taken away unless the person either is saved or passes away. As long as the name is there, you should pray for him until he is saved.

So your record book should have the following items: first item is the number; second, the date (the day you start to pray); third, the name; and fourth, another date (the day the person is saved or passes away). I remember a brother prayed for one name in his book for eighteen years before that person was saved. Many in your book may get saved within one year; some may be saved in three months; one or two may be especially difficult—but let there be no escape.

2. PRAYER IS THE BASIC WORK IN SAVING SOULS

Why should you prepare such a record book? Because there is a basic principle in the saving of souls, and that is, before you speak to a person you must first pray to God. First ask the Lord and then speak to him. It is absolutely necessary for you to speak to God on behalf of the person to whom you will later speak. If you speak to him first, you will not be able to accomplish anything.

In a certain place I saw two responsible brothers who were very zealous in leading men to the Lord. But in my contact with them, I knew instantly that something was basically wrong. They did not pray for those whom they wished to win for Christ. An interest in men void of a burden before God is simply inadequate and is therefore ineffective. One must first have a burden before God and then labor among men.

Hence, the first thing to do is to ask God for a few souls. "All that which the Father giveth me shall come unto me" (John 6:37), said the Lord Jesus. And we also remember how God added to the church day by day those that were saved (Acts 2:47). We must ask God for souls. We need to pray: "O God, give souls to the Lord Jesus, add people to the church." People are given by the asking. Human hearts are so subtle that they are not easily turned. For this reason, we must pray faithfully for a person before we speak fully to him. How important is prayer. Pray by name for those people whom you wish to lead to Christ, believe that God will save them, and then lead them to the Lord.

Whosoever is wise in leading men to Christ is skillful in the art of prayer. If one has difficulty having his prayer answered, he will have difficulty going out and witnessing for the Lord. May new believers see that the way lies in praying before witnessing. All who are wise in leading people to the Lord are also effectual in prayer.

3. THE GREATEST HINDRANCE TO PRAYER IS SIN

Special attention should be paid by new believers to reject all known sins. We must learn to live a holy life before God. If anyone is lax in the matter of sin, his prayer will definitely be hindered. Sin is a big problem. Many cannot pray because they tolerate sin in their lives. Sin will not only obstruct our prayers, it will also wreck our conscience.

The effects of sin are two-sided: objectively, there is an effect Godward; subjectively, there is an effect usward.

Objectively, sin obstructs God's grace and God's answer. "Behold, Jehovah's hand is not shortened, that it cannot save; neither his ear heavy, that it cannot hear: but your iniquities have separated between you and your God, and your sins have hid his face from you, so that he will not hear" (Is. 59:1–2). God's mercy and grace is the greatest force in the world. Nothing can stand against it except sin. It is said in the Psalms, "If I regard iniquity in my heart, the Lord will not hear" (Ps. 66:18). If a person neglects dealing with sin, there will be an obstruction between him and God. Any unconfessed sin, any sin which is not put under the blood, becomes a great hindrance before God— it hinders prayer from being answered. This is the objective effect of sin.

Subjectively, sin damages a man's conscience. Whenever a person sins, his conscience becomes weakened and depressed irrespective of how hard he tries to convince himself, of how much he reads the Bible, and of how desperately he holds on to the promises in the Bible and the acceptable grace of God. His conscience is like a ship (see 1 Tim. 1:19). It is all right for a ship to be old, but it cannot be wrecked. It is all right for a ship to be small, but it cannot afford to be broken. In like manner, a conscience must not be wrecked. If the conscience lacks peace, there will be a hindrance in the person and before God.

I often think of the relationship between faith and conscience. Faith is like the cargo and conscience is like the ship. The cargo is in the ship. If the ship is wrecked, the cargo will fall out. When conscience is strong, faith is also strong; but when conscience is wrecked, faith leaks out. God's heart is greater than ours; if we condemn ourselves, how much more will God condemn us. This is what the apostle John tells us (1 John 3:20).

New believers ought to see that the sin question must be solved if they desire to be skillful in prayer. Thus they should note especially the preciousness of the blood. They have lived in sin so long that they will not be able to be completely freed from sin if they are even slightly lenient toward it. They need to confess their sins one by one before God, put them one after another under the blood, reject each one of them, and be freed of them. Thus shall their conscience be restored. By the cleansing of the blood, the conscience is instantly restored. With the washing of the blood, conscience no longer accuses and one may naturally see God's face. Never let yourself fall into the place whereby you become weak before God, for you will not then be able to intercede for others. Thus this question of sin is the first thing to which you must attend daily. Deal well with sin; then you can pray well before God and lead people to Christ. If you daily remember people before the Lord with faith, you will soon win them to Christ.

This is a big test. It will test out your spiritual condition before God. If your spiritual condition is normal and right, you will gain the people on your prayer list one by one.

Pray for them with perseverance. After a few days, half a month or a month, one or two may get saved; and so on. If after three or four months, your prayers are still unanswered, something must be wrong with your prayer. So you see that prayer is your greatest test. It reveals whether you are sick before God. If so, that is why your prayer remains unanswered. If you are well before God, you will see one or two saved after a reasonable period of time.

4. PRAY IN FAITH

Once believers have dealt thoroughly with their sins and maintained a strong conscience before God, they need to be further helped to see the importance of faith.

Actually the prayer life of new believers is mainly involved with conscience and faith. Though prayer is rather profound, to new believers it is only a matter of conscience and faith. If their conscience before God is without offense, their faith can easily be strong. And if their faith is sufficiently strong, their prayer will easily be answered. Therefore it is necessary for them to have faith.

What is faith? It is not doubting in prayer. It is God who constrains us to pray. It is God who promises that we may pray to Him. He cannot but answer if we pray. He says: "Knock and it shall be opened unto you." How can I knock and He refuse to open? He says: "Seek and ye shall find." Can I seek and find not? He says: "Ask and it shall be given you." It is absolutely impossible for me to ask and not be given. Who do we think our God is? We ought to see how faithful and dependable are the promises of God.

We may have believed in the Lord for some years now, but can recall that at one time it was quite difficult to believe, for faith is based on the knowledge of God. The

80

depth of our knowledge of God measures the depth of our faith. We need to know God more that we may have more faith. Salvation is based on knowing. Now that we have been saved, have known God, we can believe without any difficulty. If we believe, God will answer us. Let us learn from the beginning to be people full of faith. Do not live by feelings nor by thoughts; learn to live by faith. As we learn to believe in God, we shall find our prayers answered.

Faith comes by the Word of God. For God's Word is like cash that can be taken and used. God's promise is God's work. Promise tells us what God's work is, and work manifests to us the promise of God. If we believe the Word of God and do not doubt, we will abide in faith and see how trustworthy is all that God has said. Our prayers shall be answered.

5. Aspire to Know How to Pray

Encourage young believers to be ambitious in being people who know how to pray. Inspire them to seek to be powerful before God. Some people are powerful before God but others are not. God listens to some and others He does not hear. What is meant by being powerful before God? It simply means that when a person prays, God hears. It seems as if God is delighted in being influenced by men. Some people really influence God. Those who are powerless are those whose prayers God disregards. They may pray for hours, but God pays no attention. Answered prayer is the test of all.

Here is a fine opportunity to test whether God is a prayer-hearing God or whether you know how to pray. Write these names in your record book and deal with them one by one before God, and see how soon God will save them.

I do not know how to say it, but I do want to instill in new believers a desire to have all their prayers answered. This is better than anything else, far better than preaching from the pulpit. We should ask God for this one thing: that He may be happy to hear us. We should aspire to be powerful before God.

It is a most glorious thing for God to be willing to hear your prayers, for Him to be able to trust you to such an extent as to give you whatever you may ask for. Let this be your earnest expectation from the very start of your Christian life. Record the names of those for whom you are burdened for their salvation in your record book and pray for them one by one. If the time seems to be overdue and your prayer is still unanswered, you should have special dealings with God. Undoubtedly something must be wrong. And this shows us the value of such a book. It causes us to know whether or not our prayers are answered. It also helps us to be aware when anything is wrong. God is far more sensitive to sin than we are. Frequently we are unaware of what God has already condemned and this will hinder our prayers from being answered.

To young believers, unanswered prayers can mainly be attributed to either a bad conscience or faulty faith. Therefore, they need to confess and to deal with their sins so as to gain faith. They must believe, wholly and truly, that God will do everything according to His promise. Then they will actually see the salvation of those for whom they have prayed. They should continually experience such answers to prayer.

New believers should set apart a definite time each day

to do this work of intercession. Whether it be half an hour, an hour, or a quarter of an hour, it must be a fixed time. For without such a fixed time, they probably will not pray at all.

6. SOME WORTHY EXAMPLES

In the following, I will give some examples of how to lead people to Christ:

EMPLOYER OF A TIME-SETTER

In England there was a woman who owned lots of clocks. She employed a man to set these clocks every day so they might give the same time. She was also a person who interceded for others in prayer and kept a record book. One day she suddenly remembered the time-setter. This man came to her house every day, and yet she had never once mentioned his name before the Lord nor had she ever prayed for him. She felt the Lord had put the name of that time-setter in her heart, so she wrote it down in her book. She began to pray for him, saying, "O God, this man comes to set my clocks; now I ask Thee to let me set his soul right." She prayed daily for him.

At first she did not speak to him, but gradually she began to talk with him. Whenever he was talked to, he always said yes, yes, though he was not at all moved. This continued for fifteen months until at length his soul was set right.

Concerning praying for souls, we have to spend time before God remembering these souls continuously and mentioning their names one by one. The time between the first prayer and the answer may vary, but we must pray until they are saved.

A STOKER

Also in England there was once a stoker who fed the furnace on a boat. His face and even his body were covered with black from day till night. One day he was saved. He asked the one who led him to Christ what was the first thing he should do for Christ. He was told to pray for one of his fellow stokers, for whichever one the Lord impressed upon his heart. There were more than ten stokers with whom he worked, but there was one whom he remembered especially. So he prayed for that one day and night.

Somehow this was discovered by the friend for whom he was praying; at first the friend was quite annoyed. But when an evangelist came to town, the prayed-for friend stood up, asking, "Can I be saved too? I want to be saved." The preacher asked him why he wanted to be saved. "Because a man is always praying for me, so I want to be saved," answered the stoker. Thus one stoker led another to the Lord.

A SIXTEEN-YEAR-OLD BOY

There was a sixteen-year-old boy working as a copyist in an architectural firm. In the firm was a chief engineer who had such a bad temper that everyone was afraid of him. After this boy was saved, he learned the lesson of prayer. So he prayed daily for the chief engineer, though he dared not preach the gospel to such a big man. Not long afterwards, the chief engineer came over to the boy and asked, "Tell me why, among over two hundred people in the firm, only you are different." That engineer was middle-aged while the boy was only in his teens. But the young boy told the engineer that he had believed in the Lord

Jesus. Right then the engineer said that he too would like to believe. Later he was brought to the church and soon was saved.

In England there were big families that often opened their houses to entertain guests. These were not hotels, but homes of high-class families who liked to have guests. Two sisters had such a home, and they opened their house to receive guests. These guests were all high-class people. Sometimes there were twenty or thirty staying with them. They observed that their guests were all worldly people who were fashionably dressed. When these guests sat around the table, their conversation usually touched upon worldly things and they often joked a lot. The two sisters wanted to correct this condition, but how? They were greatly outnumbered since there were only two of them. After deliberation, they decided to sit at the two ends of the room and join their hearts in praying over every one of their guests.

During the first evening after supper, they all retired to the sitting room. The two sisters took up their positions and started to pray, one praying from one end and the other praying from the other end until they had finished praying for all. Because of their silent prayers, the guests found themselves unable to jest and joke and talk. They wondered why. That night one person was saved, and the second night another was saved. This went on until all were saved.

Remember, prayer is indispensable. Those two sisters were very wise. Instead of sitting among their guests and being influenced by them, they sat at the two ends of the room and encircled their guests with prayers so that none might escape but all be saved.

Approach Sinners on Behalf of God

It is not enough just to pray for sinners and to approach God on behalf of sinners. We must also approach sinners on behalf of God. We need to tell them what God is like. Many people dare to speak to God but have no courage to speak to men. Young people should be trained to be bold to speak to others. They must not only pray but also seek opportunities to talk.

In talking with people, there are a few things which should be especially observed.

1. NEVER ARGUE UNNECESSARILY

In speaking to people, we need a little technique. First of all, we must not enter into unnecessary arguments. This does not mean that we should never argue, because in Acts we find several instances where they argued; even the apostle Paul argued. If you have to argue, you argue with one person for the benefit of a third person listening in. But for the one whom you wish to win to Christ, usually it is better if you do not argue. Do not argue with him nor argue for him to hear. Why? Because argument may drive people away instead of drawing them in. You need to show a gentle spirit; otherwise people will flee from you.

Many think that argument may move a person's heart. But this is not true. Argument at most only brings people's minds into subjection. Therefore, it is better to speak less words which come from the mind and rather witness more. Tell people of how you have experienced joy and peace and rest after you believed in the Lord Jesus. These are facts that no one can argue with.

2. HOLD ON TO FACTS

Another method in leading people to the Lord is to use fact, not doctrine, while talking. It is not because of the reasonableness of the doctrine that people come into faith. Many see the logic of the doctrine but still do not believe.

Often it is the simple who can save souls. Those who preach well on doctrine may correct people's minds but fail to save souls. The one aim is to save people, not to correct their minds. What is the use in having their minds corrected but leaving them unsaved?

I remember once there was an old man. He attended the church meetings regularly, but he was not saved. Though he was unsaved, yet he considered going to church a good habit. So he attended regularly and wanted his whole family to go with him. Often after the meetings he would go home and get into a bad temper. The whole family was afraid of him.

One day his married daughter came to see him. This daughter belonged to the Lord. When she came to visit, she brought her four-year-old girl with her. This grandfather naturally took his little granddaughter along to the church. After the service as they walked out, the little granddaughter looked at her grandfather and felt that he did not look like a believer in the Lord Jesus. So on the way she asked him whether he believed in Jesus. The old grandfather retorted that a child should not talk. After a few steps, the child again said to him, "To me you do not look like a believer in Jesus." This old man once again replied, "A little child is not allowed to speak." After a while, the girl spoke again, "Why do you not believe in Jesus?" This time the old man was caught. He who was much feared by others was brought to the Lord through these simple questions.

Remember, therefore, it is not a matter of preaching. This little child had a keener eye than many people. She noticed that though her grandfather went to church he was different. She said, "You do not look like a believer," and then asked, "Why do you not believe in the Lord Jesus?" Thus she led him to Christ.

In preaching the gospel or witnessing for Christ, do not be afraid to be foolish. The best brain can hardly save people. I have yet to see a good brain saving souls, for as one uses his brain he always turns to doctrine. He states the doctrine clearly but this is not the way required by the gospel. You need to know God's way. If a person fishes with a straight hook, he will never get a fish. The fishhook must be barbed so as to hook the fish. This is what new believers ought to learn.

3. MAINTAIN A SINCERE AND EARNEST ATTITUDE

In witnessing, our attitude must be sincere and earnest, not given to frivolity. We must not argue, but only tell the facts of what we have experienced before God. If we stand in this position, we will be able to lead many to the Lord. Do not try to have a big brain; just stress facts. We may joke about other matters but in this one thing we must be sincere.

I once saw a person who wished to lead people to Christ. He was willing to pray, but his attitude was wrong. As he talked of the Lord, he joked and jested along. These two are incompatible. Through frivolity he lost whatever spiritual power he might have had. He had no way tc lead people to Christ. In witnessing, our attitude must be sincere. We need to impress upon others that this is a most serious matter.

4. ASK GOD FOR OPPORTUNITIES

We should pray that God will give us opportunities to speak with people. If we pray, we will be given opportunities.

I recall a sister who led a small Bible class. She gathered many salesgirls who were unbelievers and gave them instruction from the Bible once a week. She did this for a time but with no visible result. Then she noticed among the girls one who was fashionably dressed. This particular girl was proud and had no heart for spiritual things. So the sister started to pray for that girl. After many days she invited the girl to come to her home and have tea with her. The girl expected to have a nice social visit, and so she went. But as soon as they sat down, the sister began to persuade her to believe. The girl answered, "I cannot believe for I love playing cards, I love the theater, I love the world. I am not willing to incur the loss of these things, so I cannot believe in the Lord Jesus." The sister acknowledged that such would be the case if one believed in the Lord Jesus; one would have to give up cards, the theater, and the pleasures of this world. The girl said, "The cost is too much; I cannot afford to pay it." She was asked by the sister to go home and reconsider.

Returning home she knelt down to pray. After prayer, she decided to follow the Lord Jesus. She was suddenly transformed. She did not know why, but her heart was turned. Her dress and her make-up also underwent a change. A month later the manager of her floor called her to his office and congratulated her on her change. She was surprised. So the manager told her that they had had a meeting in which a decision had been reached that they would fire her if she continued to be as she used to be for another week. She had been so arrogant, disrespectful to customers, overly adorned, and frivolous that she had thought only of herself, not of the business of the firm. But strangely, within that week she had changed. He asked if he might know the reason. The girl testified that she had accepted the Lord Jesus. Within a year over a hundred salesgirls were brought by her, one after another, to the Lord.

Some seem to be difficult to talk with. But if you pray for them, you will be given opportunities to speak to them and they will be changed. Look at the sister referred to above. She was at first afraid to talk to that girl for the latter was so arrogant in her attitude and so worldly in her attire. The Lord, however, gave the sister a burden to pray. Then one day the Lord gave her courage to speak to the girl.

Therefore, we must learn to pray and also to speak. Many dare not open their mouths to speak of the Lord Jesus to their friends and relatives. Maybe opportunities are waiting for you but you have let these opportunities slip by because you are afraid.

5. Seek Out People of the Same Category

According to our past experience, it is better for people to seek and save those in the same category. This is a common rule. Nurses can work among nurses, doctors among doctors, patients among patients, civil servants among civil servants, students among students. Work on those who are nearest to you. You do not need to start with open-air meetings, but with your family and acquaintances. It is natural for doctors to work on their patients, teachers on their students, employers on their employees, masters on their servants.

I remember there were twelve houses in a certain lane in Shanghai. One maidservant got saved. She decided to start with the first house on the right. Soon the maid of that house on the right was saved, and then the maid of the second house on the right got saved, and so on. By the time I heard of it, six maidservants had already been saved.

Let the children work among the children. It is most convenient to work by this rule of staying within the same category. Let the men seek out the men, and the women, women. I do not say that it must be so, but from our past experience it does seem to be the most effective.

New believers should know to what category they belong, then seek out those of the same category. With the exception of people being your friends or relatives or neighbors, this rule usually is both effective and conveniently applicable.

I do not say there are no exceptions, for there are some. Our Lord Jesus Himself gave us some exceptional examples. Nonetheless, this rule is generally preferable. For a miner to preach in a college is exceptional. Though the Lord does sometimes do exceptional things, yet He cannot be expected to do such things every day. For example, for a very learned person to talk to the laborers at the pier is not quite suitable. But if a few longshoremen are saved and they go out to save the rest, it seems to me to be a more appropriate and easier way.

6. Bring People to God Daily through Prayers

There will never be a time when there is no one to pray for. You can pray for your fellow students, your colleagues, your fellow nurses or doctors, and your fellow employees. Ask God to put especially one or two of them upon your heart. When He puts a person in your heart, write his name in your book and pray daily for him.

After you have begun to pray for a soul, you should also talk to him. Tell him of the grace of the Lord to you. This is something he cannot resist or forget.

7. In Season and Out of Season

Finally, I wish to mention that you are not forbidden to speak to those for whom you have not prayed before. There will be some to whom you will speak when you meet them for the first time. Seize every opportunity; speak both in season and out of season, for you do not know who will slip away. You must open your mouth regularly even as you should pray always. Pray for those with names and pray for many without names. Pray that the Lord will save sinners. Whenever you meet a sinner by chance, if the Spirit of God moves you, speak to him.

I recall a story about a British naval officer who attended a race in London. Crowds of people were there watching the race. It so happened that a middle-aged noble lady was watching by his side. He wondered in his heart if this lady knew the Savior. So he turned to her and said: "Pardon me. I have an important question to ask you—do you know my Savior?" The lady was stunned and surprised at such a question. He explained to her that the Lord Jesus was his Savior and he encouraged her to accept Him. The lady expressed her willingness to receive the Lord Jesus. They knelt down to pray and the lady was soundly saved.

Let me tell you, if we are a little careless, souls will slip away from us. May God's fishermen today cast such a fine net that no fish will slip away.

Practice is Required

Each time you try to lead a sinner to the Lord, you must treat it as a case to be studied. You must be like a medical doctor who studies each and every case. You cannot give a prescription indiscriminately. Likewise, in dealings with souls you have to study them as cases. Acknowledge each failure and find out the reason for each success.

No one in the world can be an accountant, a teacher, a doctor, a nurse, or even a sedan-chair bearer without proper training. Likewise, how can we be soul-winners without first learning how to lead people to the Lord? There are many who have become rather skillful in winning souls. Such ones study each case carefully every time.

We should always inquire why a certain one accepted the Lord. Was there anything we said that made him believe? Or why did another one seem to listen so well and yet slip away afterwards? Was it because we did not use the right bait? Do not blame others for all the difficulties; rather look into yourself for the problem, as all who are skillful in winning souls usually do. If people are not saved, something must be wrong in us. We cannot sit by the seashore and wonder why the fish do not leap into the boat. We need to spend time searching out the reason why people are not saved. There is a technique in soul-winning. And this technique is learned by doing. We can learn from our failures as well as from our successes.

I can testify before you today that if you really put yourselves to the task, you will discover it is not too difficult at all. You may win many without any difficulty. Actually there are only a few types of people in the world. For each type of person, you need to have a special kind of word in order to get them saved. If you use the wrong approach, you will only cause trouble.

Once we have learned to deal with the different types of people, we will be able to deal with anyone. We will even know how to deal with those whom we meet by chance. As soon as we have an opportunity to witness for Christ, we will quickly discover what type of person he is. We will then know what approach we should use. With the right word, the man will be saved. In short, we acknowledge the truthfulness of the word that it is the wise who win souls.

Distributing Tracts

1. TRACT DISTRIBUTION HAS NO TIME LIMITATIONS

During the past two or three hundred years, God has especially used gospel tracts to save people. Tracts have several special advantages. One advantage is that whereas in speaking there is the limitation of time as well as the restriction of people—that is, you cannot speak twenty-four hours a day nor will people always be conveniently present to hear you—with tracts there is no such limitation or restriction. You may distribute tracts at any time, and people can read them at their convenience. Some people may not have the time to go to meetings and listen to the preaching of the gospel, but they can always be given a tract to read.

2. TRACTS MAY PRESENT THE GOSPEL FULLY

Often people have the zeal to witness for the Lord but are unable to present the gospel fully and completely. A good way for new believers is to choose some good gospel tracts and distribute them. This will help you to accomplish what you yourself cannot do.

3. TRACTS ARE UNAFFECTED BY PEOPLE

In talking to people, sometimes we are unable to present the gospel as fully or seriously as it should be. We are easily affected by human considerations and feelings. With tracts there is no such problem. They say what is to be said irrespective of who is reading them. When we preach the gospel, we cannot avoid being influenced by people, but preaching by tracts is absolutely above such influence. So new believers should start to sow with tracts.

4. TRACTS MAY BE SCATTERED EVERYWHERE

Another advantage of tracts is that they may be scattered everywhere. As the Old Testament says, "Cast thy bread upon the waters; for thou shalt find it after many days" (Eccl. 11:1). It would consume lots of time to speak to three, five, ten people. But when I first believed in the Lord, I distributed daily an average of one to three thousand tracts. Take a pile of tracts with you when you go out. Give one to whomever you meet. This is like sowing upon the face of the waters. If only one person is saved through those one thousand distributed tracts, it is really worthwhile

5. TRACTS ARE REALLY USED BY GOD TO SAVE PEOPLE

God sometimes uses tracts in amazing ways to save people. I remember once a man threw away a tract on the road. Another man came by. One nail in his shoe happened to stick out and caused pain to his foot. He was looking for some paper to pad the inside of his shoe. He picked up the tract and put it in his shoe. While his shoe was being repaired afterwards, he read the tract and was saved. Many wonderful stories like this can be told of how tracts have been used to save souls.

6. PRAY FAITHFULLY AND WORK SINGLE-MINDEDLY

Whenever new believers are free, they should put tracts in their pockets and distribute them. In doing this work of leading people to Christ, we need to pray faithfully and undertake the task with singleness of heart. As we distribute, we may add a word or two or we may say nothing. But we do expect to see people come to the Lord.

HOUSEHOLD SALVATION

The Promise of God

Most things have their basic unit and the unit for salvation is the household. We find in the Bible that God gives many promises in regard to His dealings with men. If we know these promises, we will be greatly benefited; otherwise, we will suffer loss. The promise which God gives concerning salvation takes a household, not an individual, as the basic unit. New believers should be reminded of this, for it will solve many problems and give them great benefit.

The Unit of Salvation

When the Bible speaks of eternal life, it always takes an individual as the unit; never does it take a household as the unit. But when it deals with salvation, it actually takes the household instead of the individual. We must see that the unit of salvation is the household while that of eternal life is the individual.

We wish to spend some time in searching a number of Scripture verses so as to convince ourselves of the fact that salvation is for the household. Then we will be able to come to God and plead for households according to His Word.

Our Course

We do hope that in the future we will not need to spend lots of time trying to save the children born in our midst, trying to bring our second generation back from the world. All who are born into our homes according to the flesh should also be born into our homes according to the Spirit. We should not lose them year after year and then have to save them back afterwards. It is not enough for us just to bring them into the world; we must also bring them to the Lord.

If brothers and sisters are convinced of this, we will have as many children saved as are born to us. The Lord has given them to us. How can we allow them to go away without being saved? Must we save them back from the world? We will waste a great deal of time if we let all these small fish go back to the sea and try to catch them afterwards. No, these small fish must stay with the larger ones. Whether or not the church has a second generation depends largely on whether or not our children belong to the Lord.

I do desire that brothers and sisters may see the significance of this matter. If we lose those born to us, very soon we will not have a second generation. But if generation after generation continues, along with new additions from outside, then the church will become exceedingly strong.

The basic principle of the Bible is that God's salvation is for the household. Let us now examine the proofs in both the Old and New Testaments.

Old Testament Examples

1. THE WHOLE HOUSE ENTERED THE ARK

"And Jehovah said unto Noah, Come thou and all thy house into the ark" (Gen. 7:1).

"While the ark was a preparing, wherein few, that is, eight souls, were saved through water" (1 Pet. 3:20b).

The ark was not for one person; it was for the whole house. The Bible affirms that the man Noah was righteous before God, but nowhere does it record that Noah's sons and daughters-in-law were righteous. Noah alone was referred to as a righteous man. Yet when God prepared His salvation for Noah, He commanded all his house to enter into the ark. The ark used the household instead of an individual as its unit.

A new believer should bring all his house to the ark. You may pray: "Lord, I have trusted in You. Now I ask You to bring my whole house in because You have said that all my house may come in." God will respect your faith and bring in your whole house.

2. A WHOLE HOUSE WAS CIRCUMCISED

"And he that is eight days old shall be circumcised among you, every male throughout your generations, he that is born in the house, or bought with money of any foreigner that is not of thy seed. He that is born in thy house, and he that is bought with thy money, must needs be circumcised: and my covenant shall be in your flesh for an everlasting covenant" (Gen. 17:12–13).

God called Abraham and covenanted with him to make him and his house His own people. The sign of the covenant was circumcision. All who were circumcised belonged to God; all who were not circumcised were not of God. God commanded Abraham to have his whole house circumcised—those who were born in his house as well as those who were bought with his money. So the promise regarding circumcision was not given to Abraham alone; it was given to the house of Abraham. Circumcision had the household as its unit of operation. God's promise was for the whole house of Abraham, not just for Abraham himself.

3. A Paschal Lamb for Each House

"Speak ye unto all the congregation of Israel, saying, In the tenth day of this month they shall take to them every man a lamb, according to their fathers' houses, a lamb for a household: . . . And they shall take of the blood, and put it on the two side-posts and on the lintel, upon the houses wherein they shall eat it" (Ex. 12:3, 7).

The paschal lamb was definitely for the household, not for an individual. Thus we are shown how important is the household in the sight of God. The lamb was slain not for one person but for the whole house, and its blood was put on the door that the household might be preserved. The angel, the destroyer, would pass over the house which had the blood on the door.

How marvelous that the salvation which the Lord Jesus Christ has prepared is like the paschal lamb for the whole house. It is for the household to eat the lamb and to apply the blood. The whole family together receives the salvation of the Lord.

4. THE PRIESTHOOD IS FOR THE HOUSEHOLD

The priesthood which God promised was also for the household. "And Jehovah said unto Aaron, Thou and thy sons and thy fathers' house with thee shall bear the iniquity of the sanctuary; and thou and thy sons with thee shall bear the iniquity of your priesthood" (Num. 18:1).

"And this is thine: the heave-offering of their gift, even all the wave-offerings of the children of Israel; I have given them unto thee, and to thy sons and to thy daughters with thee, as a portion for ever; every one that is clean in thy house shall eat thereof" (Num. 18:11). God gave all the wave-offerings of the people to the house of Aaron, not just to Aaron himself, for the whole household was accepted by God. The house of Aaron, not Aaron alone, was appointed to be priests. The priesthood was within the house.

5. A HOUSEHOLD SAVED UNDER A SCARLET CORD

"And it shall be, that whosoever shall go out of the doors of thy house into the street, his blood shall be upon his head, and we shall be guiltless: and whosoever shall be with thee in the house, his blood shall be on our head, if any hand be upon him" (Josh. 2:19).

"And the city shall be devoted, even it and all that is therein, to Jehovah: only Rahab the harlot shall live, she and all that are with her in the house, because she hid the messengers that we sent" (Josh. 6:17).

In the case of Rahab the harlot, the whole house was also saved. Why? Because she hid the messengers. God gave her a sign—she must bind the scarlet cord on her window; all who were in the house would then be spared from slaughter. The rest of the inhabitants of Jericho were all killed. Salvation was in the scarlet cord, but this salvation saved not only Rahab but also her house.

So the scope of salvation is pretty clear—it is the household. In chapter two of Joshua, we see the promise; in chapter six, the practice. As the promise was, so was the practice. The whole house of Rahab was therefore saved.

6. BLESSING UPON THE HOUSE

"And the ark of Jehovah remained in the house of Obed-edom the Gittite three months: and Jehovah blessed Obed-edom, and all his house" (2 Sam. 6:11).

The blessing of Jehovah in the Old Testament was also for the household. As the ark remained in the house of Obed-edom, the Lord blessed him and all his house. The unit for blessing is the house, not the individual.

I would like to use this opportunity to mention that not just in this matter of salvation, but in many things in both the Old and the New Testaments the household is taken as the basic unit. God's children, especially the heads of families, should notice that God's dealing with men is on the unit of the house. If you are ignorant of this principle, there is much that you will miss. As head of the family, you should lay hold of this principle and pray: "Lord, You have told me that You are not only dealing with me but with my house as well. Therefore, I ask You to save my household."

Not only the head of the family can claim this promise; other members of the house can also lay hold of the father's house and claim the promise. Rahab was not head of the family; yet it was she who laid hold of God and thus the whole house was saved through her. If you are the head of the family, good, because as head you can represent the family in claiming the promise. However, you who are not the head of the family can also rise up in faith and claim God's promise, as Rahab did, for the whole house: "Lord, I pray that You will lead my whole house to Yourself that they may be blessed by You."

7. REJOICE WITH THE HOUSEHOLD

"And there ye shall eat before Jehovah your God, and ye shall rejoice in all that ye put your hand unto, ye and your households, wherein Jehovah thy God hath blessed thee" (Deut. 12:7).

"And thou shalt bestow the money for whatsoever thy soul desireth, for oxen, or for sheep, or for wine, or for strong drink, or for whatsoever thy soul asketh of thee; and thou shalt eat there before Jehovah thy God, and thou shalt rejoice, thou and thy household" (Deut. 14:26).

Do you see how God told the Israelites they were to live before Him? Each household was to eat and drink and rejoice before God. In other words, the blessing is for the house, not for the individuals. You and your household should rejoice together in the blessing of the Lord.

New Testament Examples

1. THE HOUSE OF ZACCHAEUS

What about Zacchaeus? "And Jesus said unto him, Today is salvation come to this house, forasmuch as he also is a son of Abraham" (Lk. 19:9). How wonderful it is that the New Testament proclaims the same principle. We usually think of salvation as coming to the individual. Perhaps many have preached that way. But the Lord declares that "salvation has come to this house."

When you go out to preach the gospel, you should pay attention to household salvation. Do not expect only individuals to be saved. If you really believe and truly expect more, your work will undergo a great change. We want whole houses to be converted. Much depends on your faith and expectation. Should you expect them to come one by one, they will come one by one. But if you believe in their coming house by house, you will get them house after house. The scope of God's salvation is the house; let us not reduce that scope.

2. THE HOUSE OF THE NOBLEMAN

"So the father knew that it was at that hour in which Jesus said unto him, Thy son liveth: and himself believed, and his whole house" (John 4:53). He who was healed was only one person, the nobleman's son; but the Bible records that the nobleman and his whole house believed in the Lord. Although the son alone received grace directly, nonetheless, the whole house turned to the Lord. Let our request and expectation before God also produce such abundant fruit.

3. THE HOUSE OF CORNELIUS

"A devout man, and one that feared God with all his house, who gave much alms to the people, and prayed to God always" (Acts 10:2).

"Who shall speak unto thee words, whereby thou shalt be saved, thou and all thy house" (Acts 11:14).

Cornelius invited his relatives and friends to hear Peter.

As Peter spoke, the Holy Spirit fell upon them, and all who were gathered in his house were saved. This is a tremendous demonstration that God deals with households rather than just with individuals.

4. THE HOUSE OF LYDIA

"And when she was baptized, and her household, she besought us, saying, If ye have judged me to be faithful to the Lord, come into my house, and abide there. And she constrained us" (Acts 16:15). The apostles preached the gospel to the household of Lydia and they believed and were baptized.

5. THE HOUSE OF THE PHILIPPIAN JAILOR

"And they said, Believe on the Lord Jesus, and thou shalt be saved, thou and thy house" (Acts 16:31). This is one of the most famous Bible verses in Christianity.

Believe on the Lord Jesus and you shall be saved, even you and your house. I do not think we can dispute this statement. God's Word does not say, Believe on the Lord Jesus and you shall have eternal life, you and your house. It says, Believe on the Lord Jesus and you shall be saved, you and your house.

In both the Old and the New Testaments, God deals with men by the household unit. This is the smallest unit; let us not further reduce it. If anyone believes in the Lord Jesus, his whole house shall be saved. This, indeed, is marvelous. I do not know the reason, but that is what the Lord has said.

The church at Philippi began with this wonderful promise. "Believe on the Lord Jesus, and thou shalt be saved, thou and thy house" (Acts 16:31). Was this promise fulfilled? "And he brought them up into his house, and set food before them, and rejoiced greatly, with all his house, having believed in God" (16:34). How very beautiful is the picture! In the beginning the promise was given to the jailor and he alone heard it. But he brought his whole family over to hear Paul and so they all were baptized. Then he took Paul and Silas to his house and set food before them. He with all his house rejoiced greatly, for they all believed in God. So this promise of "believe on the Lord Jesus, and thou shalt be saved, thou and thy house" is not difficult to fulfill after all. The apostles gave the jailor the promise; consequently the whole household was saved.

The apostles never told the jailor anything else. For example, they didn't say, "You believe on the Lord Jesus and you shall be saved. Then after a couple of days have gone by we will tell you some more. Now you just be at rest. Slowly you should testify to your house that they may gradually come to have faith and be saved. We can assure you that this household will doubtless sooner or later all be saved."

Let me ask you: which is easier, to save individuals or to save households? Of course we do not mean that we should not seek souls one by one. But the apostles always took in households. Let us, then, not lose this privilege of bringing households to the Lord.

Let the household be the object of our labor. If we aim at the household, we shall gain the household; if we aim at individuals, we will gain only individuals. God will do things according to our faith.

If we know God's way of dealing with men, we shall not suffer loss. God takes the household as His unit of operation. In gaining one person, you gain the whole house irrespective of the size of the household. May our hearts be opened by God so that we may take this stand. Let us encourage brothers and sisters to lead whole households to the Lord.

6. The House of Crispus

"And Crispus, the ruler of the synagogue believed in the Lord with all his house; . . . and were baptized" (Acts 18:8).

We have instances in the Bible of the whole house believing in the Lord and instances of individuals believing in Him. But believing by the household in those days far exceeded what we see today. God's grace can easily come to a whole household. Crispus and all his house believed in the Lord and were baptized.

7. The Promise Is to You and to Your Children

We have already seen how the door of the gospel was opened to the Gentiles in the salvation of the house of Cornelius. Now let us turn back to look again at the situation at Pentecost.

"For to you is the promise, and to your children, and to all that are afar off, even as many as the Lord our God shall call unto Him" (Acts 2:39).

The promise given at Pentecost is that man's sin may be forgiven and he may receive the Holy Spirit. This promise is to your children as well as to you. It is therefore especially important for heads of families to lay hold of this promise, saying, "To us and to our children is this promise given. It is not for us exclusively, for our children may possess it together with us."

8. PEACE TO THE HOUSE

"And into whatsoever house ye shall enter, first say, Peace be to this house. And if a son of peace be there, your peace shall rest upon him: but if not, it shall turn to you again" (Lk. 10:5-6).

When one is sent out to preach the gospel, he should enter into a house saying, "Peace be to this house." If anyone in the house is worthy of peace, this blessing will be upon the whole house. Again, God's peace is not just for an individual but for the house. May young believers seize upon this blessed promise. Thank God, peace also comes upon house after house.

9. THE HOUSE OF STEPHANAS

"And I baptized also the household of Stephanas" (1 Cor. 1:16). Paul baptized every member of the house of Stephanas for they all believed in the Lord.

10. THE HOUSE OF ONESIPHORUS

"Salute Prisca and Aquila, and the house of Onesiphorus" (2 Tim. 4:19).

"The Lord grant mercy unto the house of Onesiphorus: for he oft refreshed me, and was not ashamed of my chain" (2 Tim. 1:16).

This family took care of Paul and was not ashamed of his chain. You will notice that it was not just one member but the whole house that helped Paul.

I trust from the few chosen Scripture passages (I have not time to mention all the instances in the Old and New Testaments) we can at least be assured that the unit of

God's dealing is the house. Especially in the matter of salvation, God takes the house as the unit of His grace.

God's Unit of Punishment

Here we will find some Bible verses which show that the unit of God's punishment is also the household. As men rebelled against God, God reacted in wrath against their houses. Thus not only peace and joy and salvation are for the household, punishment is also for the household. As the blessing of God comes to the house, likewise does the punishment of God come to the house. If God can punish the house for the sake of one member, surely He can bless the house also for one person. As woe comes to the family through one man, so blessing and salvation come to the house by one member. In view of this, a new believer should learn to stand up for his house. "As for me and my house we will serve the Lord" (Josh. 24:15b).

1. THE HOUSE OF PHARAOH

"And Jehovah plagued Pharaoh and his house with great plagues because of Sarai, Abram's wife" (Gen. 12:17). For the sin of one man, Pharaoh, the Lord plagued him and his house. If God's woe comes to the household, may we not expect His blessing to come to the household too? We are not destined to be plagued; rather are we to be people of His grace.

2. THE HOUSE OF ABIMELECH

"For Jehovah had fast closed up all the wombs of the house of Abimelech, because of Sarah, Abraham's wife"

(Gen. 20:18). All the wombs, not just one or two wombs of the house of Abimelech, were closed.

3. THE HOUSE OF DAVID

"Now therefore the sword shall never depart from thy house, because thou hast despised me, and hast taken the wife of Uriah the Hittite to be thy wife. Thus saith Jehovah, Behold, I will raise up evil against thee out of thine own house; and I will take thy wives before thine eyes, and give them unto thy neighbor, and he shall lie with thy wives in the sight of this sun" (2 Sam. 12:10–11).

After David had sinned, the chastisement of God came upon his house, even that the sword would not depart from his house. David alone sinned, but David's house received God's judgment. From God's viewpoint, one's house is closely related to one's self and they become one unit. God divides the people on earth into houses, not into individuals. Therefore we must come to God by the household.

4. THE HOUSE OF JEROBOAM

"And this thing became sin unto the house of Jeroboam, even to cut it off, and to destroy it from off the face of the earth" (1 Kings 13:34). As a result of his setting up idols, God cut off his whole house.

"Moreover Jehovah will raise him up a king over Israel, who shall cut off the house of Jeroboam that day: but what? even now" (14:14). Why did God cut off the house of Jeroboam? We can only say that it was because the house is a unit before God.

5. THE HOUSE OF BAASHA

"Behold, I will utterly sweep away Baasha and his house; and I will make thy house like the house of Jeroboam the son of Nebat" (1 Kings 16:3). God cut off the house of Baasha in the same way as He cut off the house of Jeroboam, for the unit of God's dealing is the house.

6. THE HOUSE OF AHAB

I think one of the most famous houses in the book of Kings is the house of Ahab. "And I will make thy house like the house of Jeroboam the son of Nebat, and like the house of Baasha the son of Ahijah for the provocation wherewith thou hast provoked me to anger, and hast made Israel to sin" (1 Kings 21:22). Why did God deal with the house of Ahab? Because Ahab provoked God. Ahab was one of the worst kings in the Old Testament. He received the same treatment from God as the house of Jeroboam and the house of Baasha.

7. THE HOUSES OF DATHAN AND ABIRAM

"And what he did unto Dathan and Abiram, the sons of Eliab, the son of Reuben; how the earth opened its mouth, and swallowed them up, and their households, and their tents, and every living thing that followed them, in the midst of all Israel" (Deut. 11:6). The word "household" in Hebrew is the same word for "house." Dathan and Abiram sinned against God; the earth opened its mouth and swallowed up them and their households.

I am convinced that the Bible in both the Old and the New Testaments and both positively and negatively, affirms the house as the unit of God's dealing. Brethren, do you think this is true? If so, let us live carefully before God because one person can affect the whole house.

Heads of the Families

I would like to speak specially to heads of families. To the children, our words must not be too weighty. But all the responsible ones in the Bible, with the probable exception of Lydia, are heads of houses. As heads of families, they are responsible before God in a special way. What is this special responsibility? It is that they bring their households to serve the Lord.

In the capacity of head of a household, I can claim God's promise for the whole house. I may declare that my house will believe in the Lord. Whether the children have believed or not does not alter this decision, for I, not they, am responsible for the house. I should quote the words of Joshua before God and my house, "But as for me and my house, we will serve Jehovah" (Josh. 24:15). *I* choose for the family. Hereafter the world has to acknowledge that this is a Christian family, a family which believes in the Lord.

Stand on this decision and speak in faith. Do not compromise your position. Bring your wife and your children to the same position. Lay hold of this: I am head of the family; my house shall believe in God; I have decided to have a worshipping house, a house that believes in the Lord. If you declare by faith and lead with authority, you will naturally bring your children in.

I think each and every head of the family ought to gather his children and dependents together and declare to them the words of Joshua, "As for me and my house, we will serve Jehovah." If you take this position of faith, all of your house will eventually come to the Lord, for they have no escape. This, indeed, is marvelous.

We have noticed now that household salvation is in the Bible, but our experience in this respect is not adequate. Thank God, when I was in England, I had the privilege of meeting a group of brothers who also believed in salvation for the household. I found in their midst family after family of Christians. I was deeply impressed. According to our faith, so shall God do to us. As I talked with them, I was really surprised. We have the knowledge, but they have the fact.

Once I visited George Cutting, the author of "Safety, Certainty and Enjoyment." He was at that time already over eighty years of age. His hair and beard were all white He lay in bed, and his mind was somewhat dull. But when I visited him, he said to me, "Brother Nee, you know, we cannot do without Him and He cannot do without us." He was in intimate communion with the Lord. As you know, aside from the Bible, this little booklet, "Safety, Certainty and Enjoyment," has had the largest circulation. Thank the Lord, Mr. Cutting had a family of over eighty persons and all of them were saved. His sons, daughters-in-law, grandchildren, great-grandchildren were all saved. He believed in the word, "Believe on the Lord Jesus, and thou shalt be saved, thou and thy house"; so his whole house was saved.

I do hope that you are convinced of household salvation. New believers should gather their family members and declare to them that hereafter their houses belong to God. Whether they have truly believed or have not believed, whether they approve or oppose, the declaration must be made. As head of the family, you must take this position. You should hold the rein of your house that all will serve

113

God. Let me tell you: if you take this stand by faith, it shall be done to you.

If all who have been saved had come by households instead of by individuals, what a difference it would have made. Brethren, never be negligent of the children in our homes. One of the great failures of the Protestant church is in the family. They give their next generation too much freedom. Look at the Roman Catholic Church. They need not preach the gospel, for all who are born into Catholic houses are reckoned as Catholics. You do not see them preaching on the streets like the Salvation Army, and yet generation after generation is propagated within the Catholic Church. They do not stress so much on adding from the outside as on being born within. Disregarding personal faith, all in Catholic families are included in the system. Today there are three times as many Catholics as Protestants in the world. We too should be careful not to let our children leak out into the world.

If we truly believe, the Lord will work. The way is clear: God will bless us by the household. Household salvation is a tremendous principle—one believes and the whole house shall be saved. So stand firm before God that your household may all be transformed.